FORGIVENESS:
GETTING BEYOND THE PAIN

Finding Peace with God, Yourself, and Others

SHERRY L. CAHILL

WESTBOW
PRESS®
A DIVISION OF THOMAS NELSON
& ZONDERVAN

WestBow Press books may be ordered through booksellers or by contacting:

WestBow Press
A Division of Thomas Nelson & Zondervan
1663 Liberty Drive
Bloomington, IN 47403
www.westbowpress.com
844-714-3454

All Scripture quotations are taken from The Holy Bible, New International Version®, NIV® Copyright © 1973, 1978, 1984, 2011 by Biblica, Inc.® Used by permission. All rights reserved worldwide.

ISBN: 978-1-6642-5360-5 (sc)
ISBN: 978-1-6642-5361-2 (hc)
ISBN: 978-1-6642-5359-9 (e)

Library of Congress Control Number: 2021925446

Print information available on the last page.

WestBow Press rev. date: 01/04/2022

CONTENTS

DEDICATION

I dedicate this book to those living in bondage, carrying pains from past experiences, and seeking relief. I pray that you will discover complete freedom in Christ from these pains. My prayer is that you get beyond the pain and find peace with God, yourself, and others.

FOREWORD

In Jesus's explanation of the unmerciful servant he said, "This is how my heavenly Father will treat each of you unless you forgive your brother or sister from your heart." (Matthew 18:35). In this book, Sherry Cahill gets to the heart of forgiveness, not only establishing the theological and biblical foundations for forgiveness but also practical means by which to process forgiveness from the heart. If you are a person with the remnants of unforgiveness clinging to your soul, this book may be the means to the blessing of a heart free and clear. *–Rev. Gerald W. Coates, Director of Global Church Advocacy of the Free Methodist Church*

Our dear friend, Sherry, has written this compelling book on forgiveness for all followers of Jesus. Each phrase from the Lord's Prayer can be developed into a sermon. Our Lord underscored only one phrase: "For if you forgive other people when they sin against you, your heavenly Father will also forgive you. But if you do not forgive others their sins, your Father will not forgive your sins." (Matthew 6:14–15). Because we have been forgiven, we forgive 70 times 7! *–Dr. Jerry D. Porter, General Superintendent Emeritus of the Church of the Nazarene.*

In this volume, Sherry Cahill offers practical wisdom that can help readers to understand forgiveness better and encourage them to take steps to experience the freedom of living the forgiven and forgiving life. *–Dr. David W. Kendall, Bishop Emeritus of the Free Methodist Church.*

PREFACE

God called me at age thirteen to be a missionary. I was honored to serve overseas in such a capacity. This book came into being after personal challenges and an encounter with God in Africa. During my missionary service, I started working on doctoral studies, concentrating on forgiveness. My impression of forgiveness in African culture was that it could be difficult depending on the circumstances. The more I studied forgiveness, the more God revealed to me people I needed to forgive for saying or doing hurtful things. I created a list of people whom I thought may require forgiveness. Unexpectedly, my list grew long. How could it be that a farm girl growing up in a conservative area, simply seeking to serve God, would find such a need to offer forgiveness to so many people?

During my studies, God also revealed my need to redirect my life focus back on Him. I had not grasped that other things were my top life priorities until this time. For example, my concern over how people perceived me was more important than God. My children, as precious as they are, were my top priority. When relocating to Africa dependence on God for all my needs became necessary for survival. I was forced to trust God with my children residing in the United States. I remember feeling helpless, almost lifeless, and scared. I never had to depend on God for so many things before. However, I knew that God had always been faithful to me.

I took a class about spiritual disciplines and found it helpful in handling my challenges of adapting to the local culture and being isolated from family. I started to practice several spiritual disciplines, including prayer, meditation, Bible study, and practicing God's presence in my life. As I consistently performed these disciplines and opened my heart entirely to God, I found peace like never before. I experienced joy, love, security, hope, and a deep desire to learn more about God. The more I delved into the Bible; I realized how little I knew what it said. The more I prayed I recognized my need to pray more. And when I forgave people for past hurts, more situations surfaced for me to forgive. The more I practiced God's presence; I saw my need for even more of His presence in my life.

In the following months, I encountered God in ways like never before. I poured my heart out and dedicated my life to him one hundred percent! I withheld nothing from God. He renewed my mind like I never imagined. My desire for Bible study no longer seems like a routine. God created a hunger in my heart to learn more and apply it to my life. I enjoy my time alone with God every day. My heart is now full of joy. I found peace with God, myself, and others. The transformation in my life is what brought about this book. I hope that you also experience a renewed mind in Christ. I pray that as you forgive people who have injured you in one way or another, you find peace with God, yourself, and others. May God bless you abundantly as you become intimate with Him.

ACKNOWLEDGMENTS

Many people made it possible for this book to be published. The most prominent is my wise, loving husband and best friend, **Dr. Thomas W. Cahill, Jr.,** who believed in me, encouraging me throughout the entire process. He continually inspires me to study scripture and focus on holy living. His life exemplifies forgiveness to all. The book would not be possible without his encouragement, inspiration, and example to follow in forgiveness.

My three children, **Jon Cahill, Katelyn (Cahill) Thurber**, and **James Cahill**, made it possible for this book to be published. My children and their spouses inspired me to continue following God's call when I had uncertainties. Their faith in God and me during challenging times inspired me to continue pursuing God's call on my life and to see this work to completion. Each one and their spouses are a special gift from God. Their faith, prayers, and encouragement carried me through difficult times.

I wish to acknowledge these respected leaders for reviewing this manuscript and providing comments: **Dr. David W. Kendall**, Bishop Emeritus of the Free Methodist Church; **Rev. Gerald W. Coates**, Director of Global Church Advocacy of the Free Methodist Church; and **Dr. Jerry D. Porter**, General Superintendent Emeritus of the Church of the Nazarene. These leaders provided excellent insights and comments and inspired me in many ways.

I wish to acknowledge some people who have provided outstanding editing assistance in this book. First, my friend, **Marilyn Williams,** provided significant contributions as she edited this manuscript in its early stages. **Kiersten Williams** also provided recommendations and insights upon editing this work in the early stages. I am grateful for both Marilyn and Kiersten. They offered significant contributions to this work through their expert knowledge and passion to help hurting people. The book would not be possible without them. I also wish to acknowledge **Jocelyn Simmons** for the final editing of these pages. Had it not been for her expertise and sacrificial giving, the book would not be possible. I will forever be grateful for these women of God and their willingness to complete the editing task of this book.

Several other people inspired and continue to inspire me to grow in my faith to the point of offering forgiveness to all. My parents, **Dale and Marie Irwin,** taught me the value of daily Bible reading and provided opportunities for me to know God as a child. My father-in-law, **Thomas W. Cahill, Sr.,** inspired me to pray more. Dad's intimacy with God, passion and practice of intercessory prayer, and dependence on the Holy Spirit are inspirational. **Pastors and church leaders** encouraged me to follow God's call when I was young and impressionable. Many took me under their wing as one of their own. My professors at **Trinity Theological Seminary** instilled in me the value and love of spiritual disciplines during my studies. Many others had faith in me, encouraging me to complete this book. Most importantly, I acknowledge and thank **God** for the spiritual transformation in my life as I offer forgiveness to all.

INTRODUCTION

Come to me, all you who are weary and
burdened, and I will give you rest.
—Matthew 11:28[1]

Mental anguish, headaches, anger, knots in the stomach, sleeplessness, fatigue, fear, depression, guilt, and shame are a few symptoms we suffer when circumstances arise that require us to forgive someone. The first reaction to the situation may be, "You have got to be kidding! I did not mean it that way! They just need to get over it! It is their problem, not mine!" This gut reaction often indicates conditions requiring forgiveness.

In the scripture verse above, Jesus calls the "weary and burdened" to find "rest" in Him. Sadly, many people never find that rest. The anguish and pain linger for many years. Sometimes people develop bitterness, anger, resentment, and negative attitudes, and before you know it, all facets of life are affected by the painful experience.

Our spiritual life is also impacted by unforgiveness. It is not easy to forgive. Still, I passionately believe God can help us move beyond the situation of anguish, releasing all the pain to Him permanently, even if the other person refuses to respond. I hope this book provides a path for you to seek and find peace with God, yourself, and others. The results are definitely worth the effort. My experiences have taught me the value of forgiveness and its significance in everyday situations. I

---

[1] *New International Version (NIV) Life Application Study Bible,* 2011, (all subsequent citations are from this version).

have peace with God, myself, and others, and I know that you can find peace in forgiveness too.

The following pages reveal practical methods to help you release your relationship pains to Jesus and gain peace. The suggestions are established from research and experiences on forgiveness and overcoming personal pain. They offer valuable guidance in seeking and finding forgiveness with God, yourself, and others. The book is different from others because it provides practical tips from a spiritual perspective. It involves calling on the power of God to overcome pain and begin living in peace.

The first chapter of this book asks whether we can forgive and find peace with God, ourselves, and others. Tough questions are asked as we work through the beginning of the forgiveness process. In this section of the book, we discuss deception and false thinking, how God makes it possible to forgive and receive peace, and the significance of having head knowledge of God's forgiveness but also accepting it in your heart. The chapter is critical in understanding how to get beyond the relationship pains and find peace with God, yourself, and others. A case study and questions are provided at the end of the chapter.

The second chapter of this work provides a dialogue on the biblical meaning of forgiveness. The section highlights forgiveness illustrated by biblical characters such as the Israelites, Joseph, the apostle Paul, and Jesus. Secondly, the conversation focuses on defining our worldview. It is significant since how we perceive God impacts our thinking about forgiveness. Such foundational understanding is helpful as we advance. The second chapter concludes with another case study and questions to consider, offering insights into how you could perceive forgiveness.

The third chapter guides readers in identifying potential persons or situations that may produce some painful emotions or memories. We create a list of people who may need to be forgiven throughout the process. We consider understanding our limitations and expectations in relationships. I have heard people say that you cannot fix the problem until you identify it. Gaining this understanding and identifying the problem people or issues is critical before continuing. The chapter wraps up with a case study and questions to consider before advancing.

The fourth chapter looks at recognizing and experiencing the power of God. We talk about our perception of God and how worldviews influence how we see and expect Him to work in our lives. Following this conversation, we talk about how to experience God's transforming power. We offer some methods to experience His power, such as praising God, reading the Bible, praying, practicing His presence, and finally, through God-given forgiveness. The chapter concludes with a case study and questions about our mindset and thinking about God's power.

The fifth chapter provides a more in-depth view of how one can experience personal forgiveness from God. There is a dialogue about Christ's death and resurrection. We discuss methods to leave the past behind and focus on allowing God to mold us more into His image. Readers are challenged to be decisive in getting beyond the current painful circumstances. Sample prayers are provided for interested readers before discussing self-forgiveness. The chapter is concluded with a case study and some questions to apply what is being learned.

The sixth chapter introduces the topic of forgiving others. There is a conversation on responding to unforgiving hearts. Here, readers discover that depending on God during such times is crucial. The next section of this chapter expounds on how God transformed my life and helped me work through painful relationships. The chapter concludes with a case study and questions to prompt further thinking.

The seventh chapter discusses how a person moves beyond the pains of the past. There is a dialogue on becoming aware of warning signs that might identify the presence of unforgiveness. The next section of this chapter provides both Old and New Testament scriptures of encouragement as you advance in mending relationships. After this section, you will discover a discussion on seeking out ministry opportunities to help others. The chapter wraps up with a case study and questions for application.

The eighth chapter brings everything together by highlighting the main points from all the previous chapters. The section can easily be an excellent tool for people who are genuinely looking to get beyond their pain. As you advance through the book, it is hopeful you will not read the book as only another leisure reading. Hopefully, you will discover the help that will aid you in finding peace with God, yourself, and others for a lifetime.

It should be noted that all scripture is taken from the New International Version (NIV) Life Application Bible. Furthermore, Jesus, God, and the Holy Spirit reference the Trinity (God the Father, the Son, and the Holy Spirit) and God's deity as noted in scripture. The objective of this work is not necessarily to be a theological book. It should not be considered an answer to all situations. Still, I hope and pray that you will receive some valuable information to assist in getting beyond lingering hurts and pains. Christ's love, death on the cross, and resurrection provide options for deciding how to live in Him. These decisions demand daily choices, whether to live with or without the pain from past experiences. I pray that you and I allow God to transform us more into His image every day, and we experience peace and rest in Him. Let us start with discovering and attempting to comprehend the meaning of forgiveness as Christ intended.

ONE

Is it Really Possible?

For he chose us in him before the creation of the
world to be holy and blameless in his sight.
−Ephesians 1:4[2]

I have often thought about how the God of the universe could love me. And I wondered if He loves me enough to forgive me as the Bible says. I see how others can be worthy of God's love and forgiveness, but not me. Why would He love this farm girl from southern Indiana? How could I, of all the people in the world, be worthy of God's attention? Have you ever felt this way? Many people struggle with accepting the same. They wonder how they could be worthy of receiving God's love, mercy, and forgiveness.

I struggled with this for many years, although I accepted Christ in my life as a teenager. In my mind, I knew that God loves and forgives me, but it had not been acknowledged in my heart. Of course, I would never admit this at the time. It was so difficult to wrap my mind around that kind of love. I read many books as I struggled to understand this great love of God for me. Some were inspirational, while others offered practical help. I read some books on God's existence and His love. I read stories of people who seemed to have it all together on their thinking about God. As I read these books, I was hoping for some miracle to

---

[2] *(NIV) Life Application Study Bible.*

happen in my life too. If they had it all together, I could read the books, apply the information, and be all set with God. However, as you see in the following paragraphs, my learning about God's forgiveness and love was never enough.

Deception and False Thinking

For years I lived under this false thinking and deception. I now recognize this thinking was not taught to me by my parents, friends, or others; it was a mindset that Satan put in my head. After all, I was brought up in a Christian home, attended church, and had not committed unforgivable sins, so why should God spend time on me? I thought of all the other people in the world who needed God much more than me. I considered the starving people in Africa. I thought of people living in the jungles of the Amazon who have never had the opportunity to hear of God. I thought of people who committed the sins mentioned in the Bible, such as murder and revenge. I was deceived into believing in my head that God could love me, but my heart had not genuinely accepted His love and forgiveness.

I realize today that Satan had deceived and fooled me to think such! If Satan could deceive me into believing I cannot receive God's love, then I would never truly accept it in my heart or build a relationship with God. I would be stuck in the sense of only understanding His love but not experiencing it. It would mean Satan could keep control of my heart as long as I kept this mindset. I learned early in life I could not ride the fence when it comes to God; I am either on God's side or Satan's side. I always felt apprehensive about forgiveness and thought it could not be possible until I could get my act together spiritually. I knew there were people in my life I needed to forgive. Just thinking of them brought apprehension. I watched other people and saw how they struggled with remaining spiritual over the years, and I just assumed it would be impossible for me also. However, after many years I found this mindset to be false.

God Makes It Possible

After reading this verse in Ephesians 1:4, I realized how God could love me so much and offer complete forgiveness. If God selected me before I was born to live like Him, holy and righteous, indeed, He could show me how to become blameless and holy. As I was experiencing some recent challenges, God proved His love to me on a moment-by-moment basis. I was reminded about God's love and forgiveness for me. He was there for me when no one else could be. Today I recognize that if I were the only person on earth, Christ still would have gone to the cross and died for me to reconcile me to Himself because He loves me so much. I realize it is possible to find forgiveness in God today and every day. And, as I find forgiveness in Him, I find peace with God and myself. And as I offer the same forgiveness to others, I find peace with them too. It is the same for you too. God loves you and offers His forgiveness to you. He also wants you to show this same forgiveness to others. He wants you to have peace with God, yourself, and others. But, if we cannot accept this reality of God's love for us, it will be tough to acknowledge and accept His forgiveness. We must understand and accept God's love not only in our hearts but also in our minds.

The Heart and Mind

Before we go deeper into this subject of forgiveness, it is essential to understand and accept in both your heart and mind that God created you and me to be His holy people. Jeremiah 1:5 tells us God knew each of us inside our mother's womb. Yes, even if your parents never planned on having you, God knew and loved you when you were in the womb. When we consider that God knew us even before we were born and combine this with the reality that God created us for His purpose, we cannot refute His love for us. We can reject it, though, if we choose. But if we reject God's love, we are also rejecting His forgiveness. You and I have a choice. But, without understanding God's love and accepting it in both our heart and mind, we cannot understand His forgiveness. You and I must accept God's love for us as truth to be capable of grasping an understanding of His forgiveness.

Summary

In this first chapter, we have talked about the reality of forgiveness. We have asked difficult questions to spark our thinking to go deeper on the subject. I am unsure what lies and deceitful things Satan may have instilled into your thinking and mind. But I am entirely confident that God's love and forgiveness are real as I have experienced them in my life. I firmly believe that Satan has many people deceived. He has instilled in their thinking like he had mine that God's forgiveness and love are real but not enough for me to experience it. Satan has them believing it in their head, but they have not genuinely accepted God's love and forgiveness in their heart. But what about you? Do you accept God's love as truth? It is unquestionably necessary to accept His love as truth for you to understand how to get beyond your pain and find peace with God, yourself, and others. I encourage you to keep reading on and searching in your heart for what God is telling you. In the following case study, consider how you might respond or react and answer the questions afterward.

Case Study One

Your friend is struggling to understand if God is truly there for her. Since experiencing relationship problems in her marriage, she cannot find it in herself to forgive her spouse for the horrible things he said to her. Sleeping and eating have become a problem, and your friend is even wondering if God loves her. She feels guilty about the whole thing happening in her home. No matter what, she is unable to have peace within herself. What advice will you give your friend? How can you help her understand that God loves her no matter the situation?

My Response

Before continuing to read on, let me encourage you to take time to examine your thinking about God. Ask yourself these questions:

🤔 *Questions*

1. Do I genuinely understand God's love?

2. Do I accept and believe that God loves me?

3. Have I accepted this truth of God's love in my head?

4. Have I also accepted God's love in my heart?

5. Are there lies and deceitful things Satan has placed in my thinking? If so, what am I going to do about them?

6. How do I honestly feel about God today?

Notes

TWO

Understanding Forgiveness

Let the wicked forsake their ways and the unrighteous their
thoughts. Let them turn to the LORD, and he will have mercy
on them, and to our God, for he will freely pardon.
–Isaiah 55:7[3]

God created us to be relational people. Difficult life circumstances
may cause mental, physical, and spiritual anguish. Tensions inevitably
develop between individuals and may carry over to marriage, the
workplace, and even the church. But there is hope for forgiveness
and healing. It is essential to clarify that there are various kinds of
forgiveness: God-given forgiveness, self-forgiveness, and forgiveness
of others. In this book, we will discuss all three. The following pages
intend to offer hope and guidance to people experiencing mental
anguish, which often has physical and spiritual consequences.

This work aims to provide suggestions for what a person can do
to seek forgiveness from God, forgive others, and forgive oneself. The
following process may not be the answer to every situation. Yet based
on experience and research, the suggestions may lead us in gaining
personal victory over things that weigh us down and, in some cases,
cause physical, mental, and spiritual breakdowns.

---

[3] *(NIV) Life Application Study Bible.*

Biblical Definitions

The terms *forgive* and *forgiveness* have been tossed loosely around for a long time. If we are to understand forgiveness, it is first essential to discover the biblical definitions of these words. These definitions should help us learn God's view on the topic.

The word *forgive* is found 152 times in the Bible.[4] This information indicates the significance of forgiveness in scripture! These statistics do not reflect other words used throughout scripture with similar definitions. However, W.R. Domeris introduces us to the biblical meaning of forgiveness in the Old Testament Hebrew and New Testament Greek.[5] Let us look at his terms and definitions.

First, Domeris claims the Old Testament Hebrew word *kippur* means we protect or hide something.[6] In the Greek New Testament terms, Domeris claims there are three words to recognize the meaning of forgiveness: *apoluo*, which indicates we set something free; *aphiemi*, which signifies releasing something; and *charizomai*, indicating we are kind or polite.[7]

Logos Bible Software also provides us with some biblical definitions of forgiveness.[8] First, we learn the word *ka-po-ret* stems from the Hebrew root word for forgive and translates to penitence.[9] Another Hebrew word, *kpr* for forgiveness, translates as placating, apologizing, performing recompense, and getting things right.[10] Jesus used the Greek word *aphesis*, interpreted as delivering or placing something without charge, when He discussed forgiveness in Matthew 26:28, as He correlates His

---

[4] Logos Bible Software, *Bible Word Study Guide*, (s.v. "forgive,"). V. 9.5 SR-19.5.0.0019 (Faithlife. PC. 2021). (The count is identified in the New International Version (NIV) of the Bible according to the source).

[5] William R. Domeris, "Biblical Perspectives on Forgiveness," *Journal of Theology for Southern Africa* 54 (March 1986): 48-50, accessed January 8, 2019, http://web.b.ebscohost.com/ehost/pdfviewer/pdfviewer?vid=4&sid=8694c753-4baf-4760-a05b-5e601d0f109d%40pdc-v-sessmgr03.

[6] Domeris, 49.

[7] Domeris, 49.

[8] Logos, *Bible Word Study Guide*, (s.v. "forgive"), 2021.

[9] Logos (s.v. "forgive"), 2021.

[10] Logos (s.v. "forgive"), 2021.

teaching to His covenant.[11] These definitions indicate releasing hurts and pains to God, who then extends freedom from bondage. Keeping the meanings in mind will be advantageous as we explore some biblical demonstrations of forgiveness. We hope to gain a better scriptural knowledge of these words by viewing illustrations from the Bible.

Biblical Illustrations of Forgiveness

The Israelites

Let us first take a quick look at the account of the Israelites in the Old Testament book of Exodus. We see God's chosen ones continually struggling with faithfulness in keeping God's commands. As they strive to follow God's leading to the Promised Land, they face distractions and obstacles along the way. As you read through these events in the Bible, you will find a pattern demonstrated in the Israelites' behavior. For example, their pattern of behavior and response may be outlined as follows:

- The Israelites follow God.
- Next, they get distracted and choose to sin in various ways.
- Then, the Israelites are warned by God or His leaders about their sins and are reminded they need to refrain from sinning.
- Next, the Israelites recognize their sins and confess them to God.
- Following this, God's children seek His forgiveness and create altars of sacrifice to Him as they repent.
- Then, through His love, God shows mercy to the Israelites, forgiving their sins.
- Finally, the Israelites advance in their relationship with God and their journey to the Promised Land.

The Israelites continued to struggle for many years in the wilderness, repeating this same process frequently. The biblical account discloses the physical, mental, and spiritual challenges the Israelites confront in

---

[11] Logos (s.v. "forgive"), 2021.

staying faithful to God and His calling. Eventually, the Israelites enter the Promised Land. There are several lessons we learn from this biblical account.

First, we learn that God has great compassion, love, grace, mercy, and patience for His people. These characteristics of God are consistently seen throughout the Bible. An excellent example of these is seen in the extent God went to restore His people to Himself.

Second, we see that efforts were essential by the Israelites to restore their relationship with God. They were expected to act in response to God's call. The relationship between God and His people required both God and the Israelites to do their part. We must do our part too.

Third, we notice that God's acts of forgiveness follow the Israelites' choice to seek Him. As the Israelites seek God and repent, He demonstrates forgiveness. But first, the choice was made by the Israelites. We each have a choice of responding to God's call. Each one of us must choose as well.

Fourth, we learn of God's ability to restore brokenness when people seek Him. We live in a world with much brokenness and pain. But we must remember that God is ready and able to restore broken relationships between Him and His children. It is up to us to seek Him and ask for His healing.

Fifth, it is evident through the Israelite account that God's power is available daily as people trust and depend on Him. People place their trust in many things today. Some trust and depend on money and power, while others trust in people and materialistic items. But when we trust and depend on God, He is ready to use His power as He did with the Israelites.

Finally, we discover God's constant pursuit of His people and triumph over sin. He never gives up on us. God continues to pursue us even when we distance ourselves from Him. His love and compassion to reconcile humanity to Himself are immense.

Joseph and His Brothers

Another Old Testament narrative is that of Joseph, which is found in the book of Genesis.[12] Joseph's father exhibited his love for him in the form of a special gift of a colorful coat. But we find the jealous brothers sold Joseph into slavery and then deceived their father into believing he had died. The father mourned his son's loss during this time, and the separation of Joseph from his father was tremendously painful. He mourned the loss of this relationship too. Years later, a famine struck the land requiring the brothers to travel to Egypt for food supplies. They did not know Joseph was in Egypt and distributing grain. Joseph quickly recognized his brothers when they arrived. However, meeting his brothers presented a choice for Joseph: he must decide if he will identify himself and forgive them or just not say anything at all. Joseph selected forgiveness in the end. Some scholars, like Berthoud, believe that as the meeting between the brothers and Joseph took place, Joseph saw an altered attitude and changes in his brothers' thinking from previously.[13] I often wonder what Joseph's response might have been if he had not noticed a change in his brothers' attitudes. Would Joseph have identified himself? Would he have offered forgiveness to them at all? Perhaps the story would have ended differently. But forgiveness between the siblings occurs, although all had to overcome the past pain of their relationship. The biblical account of Joseph and his brothers offers the following insights.

The first insight is that forgiveness extends hope for mending broken relationships. God can mend our relationships with Himself and others, assuming both sides of the relationship are willing. But if one party in the relationship is unwilling to work on mending the relationship, and it may not be mended with the two parties, God can mend our hearts as we give it all to Him.

---

[12] Gen. 37-50, *(NIV) Life Application Study Bible.*

[13] Pierre Berthoud, "The Reconciliation of Joseph With His Brothers Sin, Forgiveness And Providence, Genesis 45:1-11 (42:1-45:11) and 50:15-21," *European Journal of Theology* 17, no. 1 (2008): 8, accessed March 30, 2019, http://web.a.ebscohost.com/ehost/pdfviewer/pdfviewer?vid=4&sid=d22f8362-436c-4fb4-9c5f-c81a4eda769d%40sessionmgr4006.

Second, we learn that change of hearts, attitudes, and mindsets is possible with God. God can change our attitudes and mindset towards others as He heals our hearts. Again though, we must be willing to allow Christ to make this change in us.

Third, we see that God's power is capable of anything. We must not put God in a box and limit His actions. He can do anything He chooses. God's power has no limits. It is critical to understand this concept as we move forward in our discussion on forgiveness.

Fourth, we notice God delivers strength during challenging situations. Even when others cannot offer strength, God will be there for us during difficult circumstances. He will provide daily strength as we submit our lives to Him.

Fifth, we must make choices concerning painful relationships. The results depend on our choices. God would love to heal all relationship pains, but we must be willing to open our hearts and minds to Christ, permitting Him to do so. God will not force His way on humanity. We have a choice that influences the results.

The Apostle Paul

The narrative of the apostle Paul (named Saul before his conversion) offers an extraordinary display of forgiveness from the New Testament. Paul experiences a personal and extraordinary transformation in his life. Before becoming a Christian, his actions included torturing and persecuting believers, but his behavior changed to loving and passionate activities after conversion. Paul's testimony adds credibility to his statements in his circumstances. We can glean many things from his life as we look at relationships and forgiveness. Let us take a quick look at a few of his writings to establish his perspective of forgiveness.

The Corinthians. The church of Corinth was positioned in the primary trade area and was struggling with divisions and disunity. Paul encourages them to live peacefully together.[14] He was no stranger to understanding complicated relationships and disunity as he had experienced much of it himself. In 2 Corinthians 2:5–11, Paul is blunt in telling the Christians to offer forgiveness to others, encouraging them to

---

[14] 1 Cor. 1:10, *(NIV) Life Application Study Bible.*

"reaffirm your love"[15] toward each other. In both books of Corinthians, Paul repeatedly dialogues about the believers' relationship with God and how it produces unity, not division.

We find the apostle Paul talking about the Corinthian believers' purpose and their need to remain focused on God rather than themselves. In 2 Corinthians 2:14 and the following verses, we see that he encourages believers in Corinth to reconcile their relationships. Paul does this by discussing God's grace and healing available to all people. The apostle shares his challenges and is open with his listeners, stating his desire to be transparent. His transparency with the believers illustrates God's compassion and forgiveness as Paul preaches on the topic. For myself, it would be difficult to share some personal experiences with others publicly; still, Paul does this with a sense of transparency for his audience to gain a complete understanding of what forgiveness means. But let us now look at another writing from the apostle Paul and see how he addresses the matter with believers in Galatia.

The Galatians. In exploring Paul's writings on forgiveness, in Galatians chapter two, we find he promotes getting along with others by exhibiting submission, showing respect for God, and servant leadership.[16] Paul frequently demonstrates submission by elevating Jesus while humbling himself. Such behavior is contradictory to his pre-conversion attitudes and actions. An example of his behavior change is found in Galatians 2:20, when he states, "I have been crucified with Christ and I no longer live, but Christ lives in me. The life I now live in the body, I live by faith in the Son of God, who loved me and gave himself for me."[17] Humility, a changed mindset, and a new attitude demonstrate a transformation in Paul's life after being reconciled to Christ and others. There is no doubt these are the same changes we can expect when we become reconciled with God and

---

[15] 2 Cor. 2:8, *(NIV) Life Application Study Bible.*

[16] Marcus A. Mininger, "A God-Centered Ministry and Responses to Conflict Between Peers: Perspectives From the Apostle Paul," *Mid-America Journal of Theology* 27 (2016): 125-130, accessed November 18, 2019, http://web.a.ebscohost.com/ehost/pdfviewer/pdfviewer?vid=11&sid=c3f259f9-0982-493b-9bfb-a16f97775659%40sessionmgr4008.

[17] *NIV Life Application Study Bible.*

others. Later in this book, we will discuss reconciliation with Christ; but let us now turn our attention to Paul's message to believers in Colossae to determine a better understanding of forgiveness as seen in his life and behavior.

The Colossians. The Colossae church, located in what is known as Asia Minor, was confronting struggles as many churches do. These struggles stemmed from false teachings permitted inside the church, which contradict God's Word. One teaching suggested rituals and ceremonies were mandatory to gain salvation.[18] As this teaching did not align with the scriptures, the Colossae church became divided in their thinking. They became fixated on such things, and sadly the church lost their vision of God because of the distractions. Paul sees this distraction occurring and responds lovingly but firmly in his letter to them, cautioning them to remain focused on God. The apostle Paul advises them to stay away from these false doctrines and remember the supremacy of God in all things. He recognized the church needed to shift its focus back to the things of God.[19] The following verses from Colossians 2:9–12 remind Christians of their transformation in Christ and that God's grace is sufficient for all their needs:

> For in Christ all the fullness of the Deity lives in bodily form, and in Christ you have been brought to fullness. He is the head over every power and authority. In him you were also circumcised with a circumcision not performed by human hands. Your whole self ruled by the flesh was put off when you were circumcised by Christ, having been buried with him in baptism, in which you were also raised with him through your faith in the working of God, who raised him from the dead.[20]

---

[18] "The Colossian Heresy," *(NIV) Life Application Study Bible*, following Col. 1:14).

[19] Stephen Rockwell, "Faith, Hope and Love in the Colossian Epistle," *The Reformed Theological Review* 72, no. 1 (April 2013): 44, accessed February 20, 2019, http://web.b.ebscohost.com/ehost/pdfviewer/pdfviewer?vid=4&sid=08a6810e-64d2-4cac-adbb-e25cce18c293%40pdc-v-sessmgr01.

[20] Col. 2:9-12, *NIV Life Application Study Bible*.

Do you notice a similarity between Paul's teaching in the New Testament and the Israelite account discussed earlier? The Israelites also had surrounding distractions that would draw their attention away from rather than toward God. Paul recognized a relationship with God must be a higher priority than distractions around us. He recognized we must each make an effort to remain in Christ. Do not be fooled by Satan in this same way. The devil will use distractions and anything else possible to keep our focus on something that prevents us from concentrating on God. Here are some other insights from Paul's writings:

- Satan can quickly get us distracted to prevent us from focusing on our relationship with God. Concentrating on distractions removes our focus from God and puts it on other things. We must be aware of Satan's deceitfulness and avoid it all costs.
- We must resolve to forgive if we wish to move beyond our harbored pains. We have to want forgiveness genuinely. It is a choice, and we must choose to seek it. Still, forgiveness is a requirement to advance in our relationship with God and others.
- Being transparent with God and others can be a good thing. Although it goes contrary to today's culture, we must become transparent and open to God and others as He guides us to do so.
- Jesus will provide freedom from bondage when we release it to Him. We can count on Jesus to release us from the past pains. It is seen throughout the Bible, and I testify to it myself.
- Heavenly, not earthly matters must consume us. Anything Satan can do to distract us from God consumes our time and energy. We must remain consumed with God and not permit distractions.
- We must seek God and humble ourselves before Him. We see this throughout the entire Bible; God expects it of us. It is not easy to receive forgiveness without humility. God accepts no other power above Him. He is the supreme God.
- We must pursue God about relationship matters, and He is available and concerned about our relationships. Because He experienced being a human being years ago, God understands such issues.

- Christ desires to mend broken relationships. His heart is broken when we are broken. He desires peace with us and others. But God will not barge into life without our permitting Him. We are a people of free will.

Now that we have viewed a few illustrations from the apostle Paul and how reconciliation to God radically transformed his behavior, we take a quick look at Jesus to gain more knowledge and understanding about forgiveness. Jesus provides the most excellent example of forgiveness.

Jesus

You may be wondering if Jesus ever had to experience such things as forgiveness and reconciliation of relationships. The answer is yes! Jesus, while on earth, was one hundred percent human and one hundred percent God. In His humanness, Jesus, God's son, had human emotions like you and I. He did experience such relationship strains and pains, and perhaps, His pains were more than we can truly comprehend. Although there are many examples to use, we will only offer a few. We begin with Jesus's illustration of forgiveness to the thief on the cross.

The thief on the cross. Perhaps an excellent place to begin is examining some of Jesus's own words and His view of forgiveness. One such example is when He was dying on the cross between two thieves. It is indicated in scripture that one thief had remorse for his actions while the other exhibited a hardened heart:

> One of the criminals who hung there hurled insults at him: "Aren't you the Messiah? Save yourself and us!" But the other criminal rebuked him. "Don't you fear God," he said, "since you are under the same sentence? We are punished justly, for we are getting what our deeds deserve. But this man has done nothing wrong." Then he said, "Jesus, remember me when you come into your kingdom." Jesus answered him, "Truly I tell you, today you will be with me in paradise."[21]

---

[21] Luke 23:39–43, *(NIV) Life Application Study Bible.*

Both thieves had an equal opportunity to be remorseful for stealing. But Jesus showed forgiveness to the repentant thief, even while He was physically and mentally suffering on the cross. Jesus's response indicates the repentant thief will see Him soon again. However, sadly, there is no indication in scripture that the unremorseful thief would see Jesus again. Such a biblical event illustrates repentance is crucial as we consider God-given forgiveness. What is the point of forgiveness if we cannot be sorry for our sins and come in humility to Christ and repent? We cannot fool God. He knows our heart, mind, thinking, behavior, attitudes, and everything else about us. Through these examples of Jesus, it is evident that we must repent of our wrongdoing. But let us now look at Jesus's interactions with Peter on the subject matter.

Jesus teaches Peter. In Matthew 18:21–35, Jesus talks about forgiveness, and Peter asks Him to what extent he should offer forgiveness.[22] Jesus responded that Peter should forgive numerous times if required.[23] He then simplified forgiveness to Peter by sharing a story. Jesus tells Peter at the conclusion that if he refuses to forgive others genuinely, he will be treated like those in the story; He will not forgive Peter.[24] Here we are at the choice again: do we come in humility to God asking for forgiveness? If we choose to do so, we must also be ready to offer forgiveness to others.

From this teaching time with Peter, we glean that Jesus told him to forgive with all his heart genuinely and honestly, as many times as needed. Such actions demonstrate the meaning of our earlier-noted definitions of giving these things to God. We must be willing to forgive as often as needed, repeatedly. I sincerely believe we will find freedom in Christ by following Jesus's command to forgive others. But now, let us try to unravel the meaning of forgiveness by glancing at Jesus's parable of the lost son.

Jesus's parable of the lost son. Biblical leaders frequently used storytelling in transmitting messages to a crowd. Jesus also used the storytelling method. In Luke 15:11–32, we learn His perspective on

---

[22] Matt. 18:21-35, *(NIV) Life Application Study Bible.*
[23] Matt. 18:21-22, *(NIV) Life Application Study Bible.*
[24] Matt. 18:35, *(NIV) Life Application Study Bible.*

forgiveness through a narrative about a lost son returning home[25]. The story begins with the youngest of two sons demanding his heritage money. He then leaves home, wastes his money, becomes very hungry and desperate, and eventually returns home. Approaching his dad, the son admits sinning and modestly requests his father's forgiveness and placement as a slave status within the home. The father's love and compassion were so enormous that he ran to his son and offered forgiveness, kisses, hugs, and a special celebratory feast. The younger son was restored to his original status, not a servant.

We learn much in this story about the younger son. But the story also discloses the elder brother's unforgiving attitude and jealousy. We see the jealousy engulfing him as he declines to join the celebration. The father implored him to participate in the celebratory time. Still, resentment, anger, and unforgiveness prevailed in the heart of the elder son. The father was sorrowful the son would not forgive his brother. My experience of being a parent allows me to relate to this story. If my children were not on good terms with each other, it would break my heart. I can only imagine that God feels similarly toward us when we fail to forgive people who offend us. His heart is broken, and He wants to see the relationship mended.

God illustrates His love and forgiveness for His children in this New Testament parable. Our heavenly Father accepts us as we are: wicked, hopeless, and hungry for Him. As was the younger son in this biblical story, some of us are entirely desperate. But as we come to God, He cleanses our sin, transforms us, and celebrates with us. However, many people fail to respond to this compassionate, loving plea by refusing to accept God's gift of forgiveness. Such rejection of His lost children must bring sadness, grief, and a broken heart to God.

Jesus's forgiveness of the adulterous woman. One last example of Jesus we use in these pages exhibits compassion and forgiveness to a publicly humiliated adulterous woman found in John 8:1–11.[26] Some Pharisees and teachers came to Jesus, attempting to trick Him, and presented an adulterous woman they caught in action. Those who were present did not expect the response Jesus gave them. Anxiously waiting

---

[25] (*NIV*) *Life Application Study Bible.*
[26] (*NIV*) *Life Application Study Bible.*

to stone her (the expected cultural punishment), Jesus declared that if anyone there was sinless, they should go ahead and throw the stone at the woman.[27] Everyone departed, leaving only Jesus and her. Jesus then directs the woman to see that no one remained to stone her, then offers His forgiveness. Perhaps something overlooked in this biblical account is that Jesus requests her to stop sinning.[28] Christ forgives the woman but demands behavioral change as He teaches her and us a lesson on forgiveness. We should expect no different. If we are sincere about God and come in genuine humility to seek forgiveness, He does not expect us to return to doing the same things again. These illustrations from Jesus offer several notable items about forgiveness. The following is an outline of these items.

First, we see that Christ illustrates His immense love for humanity, even while enduring great pain. He never gives up on us. His love is eternal. It is critical to understand God's love for us.

Secondly, we discover that humility before God and showing remorse for sins are relevant to salvation. It is evident from the biblical examples that Jesus requires humility and repentance from us. We must humble ourselves before the God of the universe.

Third, it is evident that Jesus displayed and valued love, peace, forgiveness, and reconciliation. It should be no secret that God's love is so great for us. After all, God's purpose for sending Christ to earth was to bridge the gap between God and man after Adam and Eve sinned.

Fourth, our forgiveness of others must be genuine and from the heart. We cannot fool God. Perhaps we can fool others here on earth. However, when we individually stand before God on judgment day, each one of us must answer for our actions, behaviors, and attitudes. Our forgiveness of others must be genuine.

Fifth, we must forgive as many times as necessary. We must not put limits on forgiveness. Our humble attitude toward others should prevail over unforgiveness. We learn this from Jesus's example.

Sixth, we should stop living carelessly on our own resources and seek God for forgiveness. We only find true satisfaction in Christ. We need God and must rely on Him as we seek forgiveness.

---

[27] John 8:7b, *(NIV) Life Application Study Bible.*
[28] John 8:11, *(NIV) Life Application Study Bible.*

Seventh, we learn that Jesus Christ is ready and waiting with open arms for us to return to Him. We must select to receive His forgiveness. It is our choice. But we should remember that whatever choice we make, we must face the consequences of it.

Eighth, it is important to note we should rejoice with those who return to Christ. It is an extraordinary event for which to be happy. Any reconciliation of God and man should bring joy to our hearts.

Ninth, we discover that jealousy and pride are obstacles to humility and obstruct forgiveness. We must repent of these sins for humility to be present. Humility cannot come without first relinquishing our pride and jealousy.

Tenth, we see that God knows our hearts and behaviors; we cannot trick Him. God knows and sees everything. He knows what we think and sees what we do. Who are we to think we can trick the God of the universe?

Finally, it is critical to note that God expects behavioral change following forgiveness. In all accounts of Jesus ministering to people while on earth, He always required them to change from their sinful habits. Their speech was not enough; He needed to see behavioral change.

The above illustrations provide a clear biblical understanding of forgiveness. Each example identifies the need to go the extra mile and seek peace with God, yourself, and others. Still, since we come from differing life experiences, we have various views of God and forgiveness. Therefore, we must consider individual perspectives of forgiveness as it influences our actions and thinking of God, others, and how we respond.

Worldview and Perspectives

As a child, I was unaware that the things taught to me and the learning methods utilized helped shape my current worldview and perspectives. I did not know that how I was taught to perceive love impacts my current perspective of love. When I was younger I did not understand how I learned to perceive fear and its influence on my Christian life and perspectives of God and others. Growing older and experiencing life brings more ways for shaping our mindset and worldviews. These worldviews often change as we experience life. In 2017, researchers discovered promising outcomes on the development of worldview.[29] They concluded children whose confidence develops and who are encouraged in their personal suggestions, ideas, and resolutions, tend to grow and perform more positively.[30] In other words, these children perform better overall in life with relationships. But what if we did not have such positive reinforcement and encouragement as a youngster, and our worldview is not healthy?

In some cultures it is customary to resist disputes to gain accord in the community.[31] Individualism permeates the Western culture creating a mentality that living an isolated life is proper. But living in isolation opposes living together in harmony with God and others.[32] These mentalities can result in someone living alone with mental anguish. We must ask whether we believe it to be spiritually, physically, and mentally healthy to carry unresolved strife throughout life? These learned response methods from childhood, life experiences, and culture may not necessarily be ways God wishes for us to respond. It is essential to determine whether our worldview aligns with God's view of forgiveness, as defined earlier in this chapter. It may be beneficial to take a few moments and consider how you process things.

Summary

In this second chapter, we discovered biblical definitions of the term forgive. We have viewed a few biblical examples of forgiveness. These examples included the Israelites, Joseph, the apostle Paul, and Jesus. We

---

[29] Kyla Haimovitz and Carol S. Dweck, "The Origins of Children's Growth and Fixed Mindsets: New Research and a New Proposal," *Child Development* 88 no. 6 (2017): 1849, https://doi.org/10.1111/cdev.12955.

[30] Haimovitz and Dweck, 1849.

[31] John C. W. Tran, *Authentic Forgiveness* (Global Perspectives Series), (Langham Creative Projects, Canada: Langham Publishing, 2020), chap. 2, Kindle.

[32] Tran, chap. 2.

learned the value of letting go and releasing our relationship pains to God. Additionally, we conversed about how worldview and perception influence current methods of behavior. Remember our discussion in the first chapter about how Satan can plant untruthful ideas in our minds? It is critical at this point to examine your mindset to determine if Satan has deceived your thinking as he did mine.

Before going on to the next section, I encourage you to think about your current mindset and worldview today. You will find two ways to apply what you have learned in this chapter. First, read the following case study and think about how you would respond. Write down your response in the space provided. After you finish the case study, read and answer the questions. Finding such answers is essential to moving on through the next steps of forgiveness. But do not be discouraged! God can transform our minds and behavior as He did with Paul and numerous others.

Case Study Two

A close friend of yours has been going through a tough time. He has said some very hurtful things to you. You have never heard anything like this from him before. But it has offended you greatly. You have been struggling to sleep and eat well. You are not sure your relationship will ever be the same if this is not resolved between the two of you. You are not even sure if he realizes he offended you. Since you are a compassionate person, you do not wish to impose on your friend's time; still, you are hurting inside and have been deeply wounded. Even if you approach him, you are unsure if you can ever forgive him for what he said to you. Still, you remember that God asks us to forgive others for Him to forgive us. What will you do as you think about how to approach the issue? Be very specific and write your response in the space provided.

My Response

I encourage you to think about each of the following questions regarding your childhood and teen years, then move on to the questions about today.

⁇ *Questions*

Childhood/Teen Experience

1. Was I permitted to provide my opinion/insight about situations?

2. Did I receive encouragement or scorn when giving my input?

3. As a youngster, was I encouraged or discouraged to discuss problems?

4. What happened if others did not agree with my opinion?

5. What things from my child/teen experience do I appreciate? What things do I wish to forget?

Today

6. Do I embrace pain stemming from my child/teen years?

7. Do I usually focus on hope and finding the good in people, or do I focus on negative things?

8. Are the people surrounding my life encouraging or discouraging?

9. Is Satan deceiving me or my thinking in any way?

10. What are some things I would like to change about my thinking patterns? Am I willing to make changes in my thinking?

11. How does my view of forgiveness compare to God's?

Notes

THREE

Examine the Situation

Examine yourselves to see whether you are in the faith...
–2 Corinthians 13:5a[33]

Now that we have a basic understanding of forgiveness, it is time to examine our situations. If we are genuinely honest with ourselves, we will acknowledge facts about our physical, mental, and spiritual condition. Think right now about how your body feels when we talk about forgiveness. Is your body showing signs of stress? Is your mind feeling bogged down? Where are you spiritually; are you connected to God or feeling isolated? You will find aids in the following pages to help you assess your circumstances. First, we create a list followed by suggestions to help narrow down people or situations that require forgiveness. Following this section of the chapter, we will find an opportunity to identify specific incidents creating tension in these relationships. Next, there is a dialogue on identifying limitations and expectations. The chapter concludes with a summary, case study, and questions to think about before advancing.

It must be clearly stated that confronting issues about forgiving myself, others, or stressful situations and moving ahead may not be a simple task. Honestly, it can be challenging, depending on the circumstances and one's personality. The forgiveness process can take

---

[33] (NIV) Life Application Study Bible.

relief at this point, relief that these things no longer hold dominion over you.

Identify Limitations and Expectations

One of the most difficult challenges in the process of forgiveness, especially to us who like to be in control of things, is recognizing our limitations and expectations. We desire the best and wish to resolve these things once and for all. However, many of these things are out of our control. We must not forget that we are only human. We cannot control how others think or behave, although sometimes we wish we could! People will be people; they will be who they are. People will act the way they want to, think the way they desire and will say and do hurtful things to us. Even though we cannot control others and their actions, we can choose our thoughts, responses, and behaviors.

Identifying Limitations

It is essential at this point to identify things in your life that are out of your control. Here are a few items to help you recognize such things:

- **Physical Limitations**. Due to geographical distance, death, or other reasons, I cannot connect face-to-face with some people causing me pain. I must accept this as a limitation.
- **Mental Limitations.** I cannot truly grasp how people think or why they think the way they do. I cannot change this. I cannot read minds or entirely understand their worldview as I did not live their lives. I must accept this as a limitation.
- **Spiritual Limitations.** People are at different spiritual levels. Some are Christians; others proclaim Christianity while not behaving in what we perceive as appropriate Christian behavior. I must accept and recognize that I do not know the spiritual maturity level of others, and I cannot change this. I am limited to such knowledge.

- **I may not be right.** For some people, this is tough to accept. You and I have met people who are always right about things. Are you a person who perceives you are always right? Think again; you are not always right about everything since you are human. Everyone makes mistakes; get over it, move on. We learn from our mistakes. This limitation exists because of our humanity.

Now that we have thought about our limitations, we must also consider our expectations of others. Although they can be intricately connected to our limitations, we must take time to ponder what we honestly expect from other people.

Identifying Expectations

All of us have probably experienced disappointment in others. I never thought my friend would treat me that way! How could they do that to me? Often, we do not expect people to respond or react to situations the way they do. Sometimes, we term it as "they snapped." Have you ever been there? Or perhaps you have observed someone in this situation. It is unsettling to us. If we were the ones who "snapped," we may wonder why we reacted that way when we have never reacted like this before. We still expect ourselves or others to respond in specific ways no matter the situation. Here are some thoughts to help you identify what your expectations are:

- **Physical Expectations.** Ask yourself, how do I expect people to respond to me? Do I anticipate them responding by punching me in the face or stomping their feet? Do I believe they will stay quiet and not say anything? Do I expect them to withdraw physically? Do I anticipate crying or harsh words? What about nonverbal reactions? What looks will I receive from them? What physical (verbal and nonverbal) expectations do I have of people?
- **Mental Expectations.** Do I anticipate others will hold a grudge against me? Should I expect them to be distant or

distracted mentally when we talk again? What about trust? Do I expect them to trust me? How can I anticipate them responding the next time mentally compared to our previous encounters?

- **<u>Spiritual Expectations.</u>** Spiritual expectations may be the most challenging for Christians to accept. We have specific ways we believe others should behave as Christians. We expect all believers to be on the same level that we perceive them to be. Sometimes we think churches, organizations, or group leaders should have a deeper spiritual maturity level than others. It may be accurate for some, but certainly not for all. These are our spiritual expectations of others.

What expectations do you have of others? The central point in understanding our expectations and limitations is that we cannot change some things. We must realize this if we are to advance in our relationships and overcome past pains and injuries. It is tough to move beyond these injuries until we understand this and move forward in the forgiveness process. The fantastic news is that we have hope in Jesus, and He is quite capable of transforming our thinking and behavior. In the next chapter, we look at the power we find in God and how it can help us when we cannot even help ourselves.

Summary

This third chapter has discovered valuable information as we pursue forgiveness and find peace with God, ourselves, and others. We started by investigating our situation. To do this, we created a list of potential people and circumstances which may have stimulated memories of past injured emotions or relationships. After completing this list, there was a dialogue on admitting our humanness by understanding our physical, mental, and spiritual limitations. Our discussion then extended to expectations of ourselves and others.

God is our creator, and He is amazingly capable of transforming and changing us more into His image despite our expectations, limitations, and humanity. I hope you are beginning to recognize and concentrate daily on God as you allow Him to permeate your life and transform you. You may find that God is teaching you to create new expectations and goals in life. In the next chapter, we will glance at tapping into God's power as we walk through this process. But before moving on, it is time to apply what we have learned in this chapter. First, read the case study and write down your response in the space provided. After you have completed your response to the case study, read the questions, and as you think about each one, write down your responses.

Case Study Three

As Suzanna made her list of people she needed to forgive, she noticed several people on her list that surprised her. One is her former Sunday School teacher. Her teacher had a falling out with the pastor and board members and decided to leave the church. She no longer wants anything to do with the church, its people, or God. It is heartbreaking to Suzanna. The Sunday School teacher strongly influenced her choice to be a Christian and mentored Suzanna during her early years. Suzanna wondered how her teacher could have nothing to do with God after being a faithful Sunday School teacher for so many years? Suzanna would never expect a person of such dedication to God could leave it all behind. Suzanna is experiencing some bitter feelings toward her former teacher and is unsure if she can forgive her. Considering spiritual, physical, and mental limitations and expectations, write down advice for Suzanna.

My Response

Questions

1. Did I make a list of people who may have created painful experiences for me?

2. Was I able to narrow the list down to those who certainly created negative emotions?

3. What are my physical, mental, and spiritual limitations?

4. Have I accepted these limitations and things I cannot change?

5. Have I owned up to my expectations of myself and others?

6. Are there things that I can change?

7. Am I willing to change and explore new expectations?

8. How do I see God working in my life right now as I work on my list?

Notes

FOUR

Recognizing and Experiencing the Power of God

Great is our Lord and mighty in power;
his understanding has no limit.
—Psalm 147:5[34]

I invited Christ into my heart at age thirteen. I continuously discover more about God's power on my daily journey in Him. Learning to forgive myself and others from painful experiences only transpired through God's power. I could never have advanced beyond these hurts and pains without His transforming power in my life. Now I sleep well and awake with incredible freedom from pain, resentment, bitterness, and anger created from past circumstances. The process persistently brings peace to my life. What about you? Do you recognize God's power in your life? What are your expectations of God? Before we consider anything further, it is critical to consider how we view God and His power. Our perceptions and expectations of God may distort how we perceive God and view Him helping us with relationship pains.

---

[34] *(NIV) Life Application Study Bible.*

Identifying My Perspective of God's Power

It is essential to consider our perspective of God as we pursue Him and desire to experience His power personally. We must recognize our view of Him could influence our perception of God's involvement with us. The first chapter of this book tackled whether it is possible to forgive. We examined our thinking of God's love and learned how critical it is to accept Christ's love in our head and heart. The second chapter talked about worldviews and our perspectives, and in the third chapter, we discussed our expectations and limitations. These things are formed throughout our lives. Learning and life experiences are intricately intertwined with our current view and expectation of God's power. It is critical to understand that our viewpoints of God affect our thinking about His ability and power to handle difficult situations we confront.

A simple example may help clarify how perspectives and expectations influence a person's view of God. I used to picture God with a whip in His hand, waiting to punish me for my mistakes. I also thought He became happy when I kept the rules. The Ten Commandments were only a few of the rules, not including others required by people. Some of you know what I mean, and this sounds all too familiar. Consequently, I sought ways to please God and earn salvation, grace, and forgiveness.

Such thinking formed a distorted belief that pursuing and meeting these expectations would generate peace in all aspects of life. Thinking like this also created certainty that even though I was working hard to achieve such peace, there was no way to achieve it. I felt much like the Israelites wandering in the wilderness, and no matter how much I tried, I could not be successful or experience peace. I was discouraged and felt shame, guilt, and oppression, struggling to meet such expectations. I battled with this for many years, seeking to please God and others. I am not stating rules are wrong; the rules I grew up with were not bad. What I am saying is these experiences helped shape my perspective of God. I learned a lot about faithfulness, loyalty, trust, and the significance of scripture, among other things, during this time. Still, I realized recently that my perspective of God needed to be changed and adjusted as I have gained more knowledge of Him now than I had then.

Experiencing God's Transforming Power

God recently demonstrated to me His power is so much more than I ever expected. I never experienced such transforming power until I went to Africa. I knew His power existed and had seen it many times before, but this experience became personal and life-changing. When I was only thirteen years old, God called me to do missionary work. He opened a door for my husband and me to work in Africa. We prepared and traveled to East Africa enthusiastically, but I had no idea my heart and life would forever change. Such experience reshaped my view of God, but more significantly, my relationship with Him was revolutionized.

My view of God's power is vastly different now than my prior perspective of Him. What transformed my perception of God, His power, and His forgiveness? I was challenged to see God from a different perspective than my own. My whole way of life changed immediately. I found myself trusting God more than ever before and developed a dependence on Him for everything. I learned to trust Him for safety, new relationships, my family back in the States, and all physical, mental, and spiritual needs. I started understanding my inability to control life and saw the power of God in everyday life experiences. Spending time in prayer, intentionally spending time in His presence, listening, and seeking wisdom on building solid relationships brought peace. The more dependent I became on God, the more obvious I realized pains from past experiences were bogging me down, and I needed to release these to Him.

I found God's grace lavished on me, unlike any other time. It occurred by pursuing God daily, striving to know Him more personally, and desiring to represent Him appropriately through my actions and attitudes. For the first time, I experienced incredible freedom in Christ. The closer to Jesus I became, the more I realized that my Christian journey is not about earning salvation, grace, and peace. It became apparent that God was so much more than I ever expected. Christ continually conveys new knowledge to me as I open up to His guidance and wisdom. His grace is available to me in both the simple and challenging situations that arise.

I pray you understand that God offers forgiveness and grace to all based on His love for us; we cannot earn it. Because we represent Jesus, our behavior and actions matter, and obeying rules is undoubtedly beneficial. However, following rules do not establish a means to earn salvation or get into heaven. God should govern the way we live, not rules. I used to think that Christianity was an easy way to live, but from experience, I know it is not always easy. Our walk with God requires daily commitment and sacrifice. As we seek wisdom from God, grow in our relationship with Him, and allow transformation from our former person to His image, He teaches us how to respond to challenging situations, forgive ourselves, and forgive others. We discover peace with God and the abundant power available to us by responding to His teachings and direction in all aspects of life. Peace with God, ourselves, and others happens as we become transparent and transformed into His image. As a result of God's transformation, it becomes apparent that life is not about us or following rules; but it is about Him.

I often feel God must be saddened when He sees us scrambling around, sort of like the Israelites, seeking satisfaction and purpose from our surroundings in this earthly life. Yet, He has so much more to offer us! His power is available daily, providing us the ability to discover peace in Him. We can overcome past painful situations through God's power. As I continue to become intimate with God and tap into His power, I have found the following methods helpful in connecting with Him and experiencing His power working in my life. One such example in clarifying this point is to experience God's power by giving Him praise.

Power Through Praise

> Let everything that has breath praise the Lord. Praise the Lord.
> —Psalm 150:6[35]

There were times in Africa when I found it was difficult to praise God. The needs of people were enormous, and my heart passionately ached to help them. Sometimes I even experienced emotions of anger

---

[35] *(NIV) Life Application Study Bible.*

toward God about the situations. I could not comprehend how anyone living in these conditions could find it within themselves to praise God; still, they did praise Him. Presenting my concerns to Jesus, I was blunt and explained that I found it challenging to understand praises in such circumstances. It seemed like God nestled me close to His side and said, "Sherry, I bring them hope, and that is enough reason to praise me." My heart was stirred, yet I struggled deep within myself. It made sense, but what do they have to praise God for, I wondered? I knew it in my head but did not truly understand this in my heart. After sitting in church services, listening as the language was translated, and watching people respond to God, I started to see God through their eyes. I honestly believe God opened my eyes to see and understand how they can praise Him. I realized God brings hope to them for a better life. As I hear people singing in their native language, my heart stirs, tears well up in my eyes, and I find many reasons to praise God. Explaining what happened in my heart during this situation is indescribable, except that Jesus transformed me.

When I am struggling to praise God, I often listen to music. As I grew up in a small rural church, singing hymns dominated our worship service. I still remember many of the words from the hymns we sang. As I sing these hymns and praises to Jesus, He reminds me of His love and the hope we have in Him. Singing praises help me transfer my focus back onto God instead of the problems I face. God changes my perspective as I praise Him, and I find new strength to overcome my trials and painful relationships. God loves to hear praises from His people. Have you ever tried it? There is power in praise!

Power Through Scripture

> I have told you these things, so that in me you may
> have peace. In this world you will have trouble.
> But take heart! I have overcome the world.
> –John 16:33[36]

---

[36] *(NIV) Life Application Study Bible.*

Growing up in a Christian home, I read the Bible nearly every day. But I did not always understand meanings from the scripture. During my time in Africa, I started to dig deep and study the Word of God, and I found the power to overcome temptations and trials. You see, as I started digging into the Bible, I realized there are so many bits of help for my daily life. I found power in God's words and instructions for difficult situations. I found encouragement too. As I discovered these gold nuggets in the Bible, something interesting happened: I wanted to find more! I wanted to read and understand more of God's Word. I felt empowered by knowing the Bible and competent to respond with answers. While I do not consider myself a Bible expert, I know there is power in the scripture for you too. God instructs us on how to respond to various situations. He encourages us to be a Godly example of someone He guides through difficult circumstances. He uses my painful experiences to help others through difficult times too.

Today I am enthusiastic and look forward to picking up the Bible to read it. I am excited to discover what God desires to tell me each day through His Word. I do not know if I will understand all of God's Word before I die, but I know that the more I learn about Him, I want to know more. I find power for overcoming pains of the past, and I know you can too. I suggest you try reading the scriptures regularly. Read the Bible with an open mind and ask God to open your eyes to a new perspective of Him. I know you will find gold nuggets for your life as you deal with difficult situations and seek forgiveness. God desires you to have peace with Him, yourself, and others.

Power Through Prayer

> if my people, who are called by my name, will humble
> themselves and pray and seek my face and turn from
> their wicked ways, then I will hear from heaven, and
> I will forgive their sin and will heal their land.
> –2 Chronicles 7:14[37]

---

[37] *(NIV) Life Application Study Bible.*

How often do we wait to pray until we are in dire need of something? It is urgent then! I learned much about the power of prayer in more recent years. I had experiences when I called out to God urgently, and He answered. God responded to my urgent prayer when my husband and I were traveling down a dirt road in Africa. Heavy rain was approaching, and we needed to drive down the dirt road and get to the pavement before the rain started. If not, we would have been stuck in the muddy road for hours or longer before the rain subsided and we could travel home. I desperately prayed and asked God to stop the rain from coming. He heard my prayer, and the rains held off until the moment we reached the paved road. God always wants to hear from us, but the urgent times should not be the only time we communicate with God. I am not saying God does not desire to hear from us during such times, only that we must converse with Him through prayer often and regularly.

Someone once told me they pictured Jesus sitting in the living room waiting each day. My friend would imagine climbing up on His lap and chatting about the events of the day. They knew He would be there waiting but sometimes did not meet Him there. When I heard this, I knew my perspective of God must be distorted! I did not picture Him so loving and kind. I imagined Him stern and just. Today, I understand that God is all these things. God holds us accountable for our behavior, but He loves us too. He wants us to live holy lives and show us how to do it through His love. I have found power through prayer, as it helps me stay close to Jesus. Prayer contributes to my understanding of who I am in God's presence and recognizing His ability to see me through difficult situations.

There have been times all I could do was cry out to God within myself. You see, my heart was broken, and there were no words to match my feelings of brokenness. During these times, God reminded me of the picture we have all seen, where Jesus is carrying the lamb in His arms. He reminded me that I am that lamb, and I need to allow Him to carry me through the difficult times. And as I cried out to Jesus, I found peace in my heart. There have been other times I struggled to praise God. As I talked to God about it, I communicated my feelings to Him. I can tell you God is my best friend. My relationship with

Him is a daily one. I interact with God often throughout the day as I do with my husband. Think about it for a moment. If you do not talk to your spouse for an extended time, does distance develop between you? Yes! It is the same for our relationship with God. When we do not communicate with God distance also occurs.

I have found that communication with God (prayer) is like many other relationships. I need to listen to Him, and He listens to me. He is patient with me and hears my cries. Many times He carries me in His arms. God often directs my mind to scripture or songs that lift Him high through prayer. I found power through prayer: healing power for the soul, strength for the problematic confrontations, motivation to carry on, and the ability to follow His call. Can you remember the last time you spent quality time in prayer? Can you recall crying out to God to intervene? He is waiting today with open arms to receive you on His lap. Just take some time and chat with Jesus now.

Power Through His Presence

> He says, "Be still, and know that I am God" …
> —Psalm 46:10a[38]

My studies found me exploring what is known as spiritual disciplines. These are various things we can do to enhance our journey with God. One such spiritual discipline is the habit of practicing God's presence. I found this discipline to be one I enjoyed very much and discovered God's power by coming into the presence of my Lord. As I invited God to be present in more of my moments throughout the day, I found that God was there and ready to help me in all my daily situations. I discovered the power to confront complex relationship problems. As I invited God to be more involved in my life, He was happy to display His power to help me overcome difficult situations as they arrived. Knowing that He is always with me does not change my need to spend time intentionally with Jesus and basking in His presence. Although practicing His presence can be done during regular prayer time, it has

---

[38] (NIV) *Life Application Study Bible.*

been helpful to me to intentionally spend additional time with Jesus, just soaking up His presence in my life.

We need to find ways throughout each day to incorporate God into the various parts of our life. Adele Ahlberg Calhoun in *Spiritual Disciplines Handbook* says we become sensitive to God's actions in life when we take short breaks to spend time with God throughout the day, which helps us focus our mind on God instead of things around us.[39] By setting aside specific times throughout the day, we remember to come into the presence of God intentionally. When we begin to practice God's presence in our life, we find power in Jesus for daily living. Calhoun provides outcomes of practicing God's presence including, "living a new way of being by letting go of your need to manipulate, compete and control," "abiding in Christ so that you see him in those who drain, irritate and anger," and "remaining open and teachable at all moments."[40]

As I enter God's presence numerous times throughout the day, I become more aware of His involvement in my daily life. God's presence opens opportunities to experience the guidance and power of the Holy Spirit. By doing so, I am inviting God to intervene in specific and challenging situations in the day. Here are some ways I practice God's presence; I hope they are helpful to you too:

- Listening to the birds sing, I focus on ways God cares for the birds and me.
- Walking outside as I see flowers, I reflect on God's beautiful creation, and praises arise within my heart to Him.
- As challenges arise, I stop, take a deep breath, and think about Jesus's love for me and how He controls my circumstances.
- As I light the candle on my desk, I take a few moments to enjoy the fragrance, and as I breathe in and out slowly, I reflect on how God is a pleasant fragrance in my life.

---

[39] Adele Ahlberg Calhoun, *Spiritual Disciplines Handbook: Practices That Transform Us,* (InterVarsity Press, 2005), 60, Kindle.
[40] Calhoun, 59.

- Before reading scripture, I quiet myself before God, thinking of all the things He has taught me through His Word and how He continually renews my mind.
- Several times throughout the day, I get up, stretch, walk away from the desk and take a few deep breaths. With each breath, I receive them as a gift from God.
- As I hear the rain falling on the roof, I often breathe in and out slowly and thank God for Him raining down blessings on my life.

Sometimes songs of praise come to my mind when practicing God's presence. I find the strength and power to carry on through the rest of the day. These are some ways I incorporate actions throughout the day to keep me present in His presence. I hope your mind is beginning to think of specific ways you can experience God's power through staying in His presence daily.

Power Through Forgiveness

> Search me, God, and know my heart; test me and
> know my anxious thoughts. See if there is any offensive
> way in me, and lead me in the way everlasting.
> —Psalm 139:23–24[41]

These verses of scripture are some of my favorites. I continuously sense the need to come before God and have Him examine my attitudes, motives, thoughts, anxiety level and determine if adjustments need to be made. We are human and make mistakes. We naturally enjoy power and control. Still, we must be willing to give up the control to God, and not everyone is ready to let go of the reins. Still, as we come humbly before our Father, we can rest assured that He waits to hear from us and to transform us more into His image. The more we practice God's presence and humble ourselves before Him, the more we recognize our weakness and find strength and power in Him. As we seek forgiveness, we should be humble before God as the apostle Paul. In 2 Corinthians

---

[41] (*NIV*) *Life Application Study Bible.*

12:9–10,[42] the apostle reminds us that no matter what we go through, God's mercy is adequate for our needs, and when we are feeble, His power is available for us.

God is offering forgiveness to us in our weakness. Our job is to humble ourselves before Christ as Paul did and receive this grace and forgiveness. Paul found strength in giving his imperfect self to Jesus and relying on Gods' power to sustain him through his hardships. God's power is available to be experienced through our coming to Him for forgiveness. But it is a choice, and we must decide if we want this. In the next chapter, we will discuss how to first-hand experience forgiveness.

Summary

The fourth chapter zooms in on recognizing and experiencing the power of God. We first talked about our perception of God. Through this discussion, we discovered how our worldviews impact the world around us and affect how we see and expect God to work in our daily lives. We transferred our discussion to experiencing God's transforming power following this conversation. A few methods are presented to help us tap into God's power in this dialogue. We talked about experiencing His power through praise, reading scripture, prayer, practicing His presence, and finally, through God-given forgiveness. Before moving to the next chapter, I encourage you to read and think about the following case study. After doing so, prayerfully consider your responses to the listed questions. Write down your response to each one and ask God to continue opening your mind to areas of weakness.

---

[42] *(NIV) Life Application Study Bible.*

Case Study Four

Mark has been thinking of how God's power can help him overcome relationship pains. He was best friends with Jeff and Joe. But these two men put Mark in a situation where he would have to take sides and select one of them over the other. This situation resulted in injuring their relationship. Mark has been experiencing relationship pains and has been living in bondage over the situation. He tried talking to both men, but neither was receptive to his concerns, and both refused to reconcile the relationship. While Mark accepts that he cannot change their relationship or control the men's choices, he wants to be free of the bondage the situation created in his life. What advice will you give to Mark? How can he tap into God's power to overcome the pain he is experiencing?

My Response

🔮 *Questions*

1. What is my perspective of God?

2. How involved do I expect Him to be in my life?

3. In what ways am I experiencing God's power?

4. Am I experiencing His power daily?

5. Do I truly recognize the power of God?

6. Do I know and accept, in my heart, that God is more powerful than past or current problems?

7. Am I willing to release my problems to Him? Am I allowing God to carry me through the difficult times?

8. Am I pursuing God with all I have?

9. What ways help me to connect to God and praise Him?

Notes

FIVE

Experiencing Personal Forgiveness

If we confess our sins, he is faithful and just and will forgive
us our sins and purify us from all unrighteousness.
–1 John 1:9[43]

If you remember our discussion about biblical forgiveness earlier in
this book, you may recall that forgiveness signifies letting go of things
and releasing them to God. Often, we wander around, much as the
Israelites did in the wilderness, acting ruthlessly and seeking to control
things. We choose to remain in bondage to our relationship pains.
But God is calling us to Him for a time of forgiveness. What items do
you need to release to God? Only Jesus can provide peace from the
past hurts. Remember, Jesus knows your story and understands your
wounds.

Christ's Death and Resurrection

It is essential to understand that forgiveness is necessary for our
relationship with God. We are told in Romans 3:23 that all of humanity
has sinned, and we need God to forgive us. The biblical account of
Jesus's death on the cross and His resurrection afterward is the Bible's
pivotal event. Looking at the big picture, the central message of the

---

[43] (NIV) Life Application Study Bible.

scriptures (both Old and New Testaments) plays out as Jesus confronts His death on the cruel cross. It is hard for me to understand the pain and suffering He endured for me and my sins, yet the Bible tells me it is true. Christ died for my sins so that I could have forgiveness.

This biblical event did not end with Christ's death on the cross. Jesus rose from the dead and revealed Himself to many people following His resurrection. Through this event, God delivers the gift of grace and forgiveness to cover our sins. It is a gift, though, and we must choose to accept it.

I have met many people who grew up in a church and followed the rules for many years. They did good things and lived a good life. From their worldview, they are right in God's eyes. Still, they did not ask God for forgiveness for their sin, and they did not have a daily personal relationship with Jesus. Our relationship with Jesus must encompass more than rituals or things we learn. Christ desires an intimate, day-to-day relationship with us today. Such a relationship with God starts as we pray for forgiveness and pour out our hearts to Him.

Praying for Forgiveness

When we consider the leaders God chose to direct the Israelites through the wilderness, we quickly see they also made mistakes. What did they do after making mistakes? They turned to God for forgiveness and found a way to advance in their relationship with Him to do God's will. It is no different for us. Scripture indicates we are all born with sin. It is because of our humanity we will mess up at times. We must ask for forgiveness and move forward. The following verses, which are taken from the Bible,[44] tell us more about how God views forgiveness:

> **John 3:16** "For God so loved the world that he gave his one and only Son, that whoever believes in him shall not perish but have eternal life."

---

[44] Taken from the *(NIV) Life Application Study Bible.*

Acts 3:19 "Repent, then, and turn to God, so that your sins may be wiped out, that times of refreshing may come from the Lord."

Ephesians 1:7 "In him we have redemption through his blood, the forgiveness of sins, in accordance with the riches of God's grace."

Psalm 103:10–12 "he does not treat us as our sins deserve or repay us according to our iniquities. For as high as the heavens are above the earth, so great is his love for those who fear him; as far as the east is from the west, so far has he removed our transgressions from us."

1 John 2:1–2 "My dear children, I write this to you so that you will not sin. But if anybody does sin, we have an advocate with the Father—Jesus Christ, the Righteous One. He is the atoning sacrifice for our sins, and not only for ours but also for the sins of the whole world."

I hope these verses of scripture bring encouragement to your heart. Our Father is waiting now for us to come to Him. Do not delay but act today. Here is a guide to help you talk to Jesus.

- **Praise Him:** Because He is God and deserves praises. You might say something like this: Hey God, you are marvelous and deserve praises. I praise you just because of who you are. I acknowledge you are powerful and able to forgive.
- **Thank Him in Advance for Answering Prayer:** God, I know you hear and answer my prayers today. Thank you for this right now.
- **Acknowledge Your Limitations/Expectations:** Lord Jesus, I know that I have physical, mental, and spiritual limitations. I realize my expectations are not always correct. I was born with sin, and because I am human, I make mistakes. But I have faith in you. Hear my cry today.

- **Ask God to Forgive Any Sins:** God, I realize you offer me forgiveness. You have paid the ultimate price on the cross, and I accept this gift of love from you, which covers my sin. I have sinned; please forgive me.

- **Accept His forgiveness:** Lord, even though I cannot completely understand your grace and all the love you have for me through your death on the cross, I know you have given me grace today. I accept your gift of forgiveness and claim it right now. I know you will guide me in the coming days.

- **Praise God for His Grace and Forgiveness to You:** Father, I praise you because you have forgiven me of my sins right now and given me grace. Lord, I praise you because I know you are in control of my life. I praise you, God because I know you will help me grow deeper in you. I praise you, God, that I will sleep well tonight knowing you are in control of everything. Amen!

It is easy to think prayer is a complicated matter. But prayer is just talking to God, listening to His response, and acting on the guidance He provides us. Some people are enjoyable to hear praying. One example is my youngest son and his wife. Sometimes when they pray, they begin with, "Hey God." Such a simple way of addressing God helps me remember that God is that personable to me. We should address Him as if He is right beside us because He is! But now that God has forgiven me for sin in my life, how do I forgive myself?

Self-Forgiveness

Once we release things to God, Satan enjoys reminding us of our mistakes and past issues. Often, we find it easy to dwell on past experiences and carry shame, guilt, depression, or similar emotions. The truth is that God has forgiven you, and now you need to forgive yourself. How do you do this? By giving it to God. Spending time with God, just talking to Him, listening to Him, and studying the Bible will help you advance in your spiritual journey. The nearer you grow to God, the more you recognize His grace covers it all; you just need to accept it.

I could concentrate on the many years I wasted being self-absorbed and focusing on myself rather than God. I could feel horrible about this and dwell on guilt and shame. But God wants me to move forward, not backward. To advance beyond the hurts and pains, I need to focus on the future. If you struggle with forgiving yourself, here are some tips to help you out.

- Praise God for all the achievements He has helped you with in life.
- Praise God that His grace covers all your sins.
- Tell yourself and acknowledge to God that you will not allow the past to be a focal point of what you will do from this point forward.
- Claim victory over the past as you release all the feelings deep inside you.
- Remember, previous situations cannot be changed, but the future can be changed. State out loud that you are moving on and will no longer dwell on these things.
- Depend on God to help you through.
- Trust in Jesus and His power.
- Tap into the power of God with some suggestions in the fourth chapter of this book.

Summary

Gathering the nuggets from what we have learned so far, you can see we are beginning to put it all together. The biblical definition of forgiveness is essential. We have discussed the value of knowing our limitations and expectations of ourselves, others, and especially God. Adding to these things is how we perceive God and expect His involvement in life and handling our challenging situations. Tapping into His power is essential. We learned several ways to tap into God's power. In this chapter, we discovered that all people have sinned and need forgiveness. We also found God's grace through His death on the cross provides a means to receive forgiveness from our sins. I hope you have prayed for and accepted the gift of grace and forgiveness from God. However, understanding forgiveness and releasing things to Him is only part of it. We must offer this same forgiveness and mercy to others. Before advancing to forgiving others, it is essential to stop and consider your responses to the case study and the questions which follow.

Case Study Five

Sheila has committed some horrible sins in her life. Sheila also struggles with forgiving herself for the things she has done. She treated her sister poorly, and her sister mistreated her too. Harsh words were spoken between them, and they had not talked to each other for years. These experiences produced feelings of anger, resentment, and unforgiveness toward our sister. Recently Sheila attended a church and heard the message about Jesus and how He can forgive her sins. She is trying to understand how the God of the universe could ever forgive her for her sins. Sheila has read some of the Bible and understands it is possible to be forgiven for these sins. She is hopeful she can forgive her sister but is unsure what to do. Sheila desires to live in peace with God, herself, and her sister. How will you walk Sheila through this process? What should she do first, and how should she proceed?

My Response

❓ *Questions*

1. Do I understand the purpose of Jesus's death on the cross?

2. Do I accept and believe He was resurrected?

3. Have I asked God to forgive my sin?

4. Have I accepted this gift of forgiveness through His grace?

5. Did I praise Him for forgiveness?

6. Am I willing to forgive myself for past sins?

7. Am I confident God's grace covers all my sins?

8. Am I ready to move forward in my relationship with God and others?

Notes

SIX

~~~

Forgiveness of Others

But if you do not forgive others their sins, your
Father will not forgive your sins.
–Matthew 6:15[45]

Y ou may be thinking that forgiveness is not complicated. You
are correct! Sometimes it can be a simple process. Some people are
enthusiastic and eager to reconcile a broken relationship. But we are
human, and this means people have the freedom to accept or reject
forgiveness. While many people willingly receive apologies and
forgiveness, others may not. I have met people who choose to carry
such bondage throughout life, which ultimately affects their health and
spirituality. How should believers respond to a person who refuses our
forgiveness? Are we not commanded in the Bible to go the extra mile
to make peace? Should we give up?

Responding to Unforgiving Hearts

The difficulty comes when we approach someone we have an
injured relationship with, but they refuse our forgiveness or fail to
accept doing anything wrong. There are no cookie-cutter answers for
every situation. Remember, God helps us forgive others whether or

---

[45] *(NIV) Life Application Study Bible.*

not they receive it or desire to mend the relationship. As we learn to lean on God and place these hurts in His hands, we find relief from our pains, whether or not others receive our forgiveness. It is our choice. We must consider whether we will allow these past pains to dictate and dominate how we live today and in the future. We cannot control how others live and respond; but, we can select how we live and decide if these circumstances affect life today. These situations require us to pray to the Lord to seek wisdom and guidance. As I lean on God for help, I have found that He takes each step with me. I know I can depend on Him for strength, and you can rely on Him too.

Dependence on God

I have encountered circumstances with unforgiving people and others who refused to accept my forgiveness. Although I released the situation to God, something kept bringing it back again to my mind. It was as if I was trying to forget but could not get it off my mind. Satan enjoys reminding us about past injuries and getting us to focus on ourselves. It is difficult when we are trying to get beyond the pain and Satan keeps reminding us of our past. Sadly, our humanity does not easily permit us to forget past pains.

However, the Holy Spirit can help us remain focused on God and not these situations. We need not allow Satan to tempt us to dwell on the painful past. Our journey in Christ is moving forward, not backward. Following the listed steps has been helpful to me when facing such hard times in my life. I hope these steps will help you focus on God instead of the past.

- Praise God for who He is.
- Praise God for helping you overcome past injuries.
- Claim victory over this situation in Christ. You might wish to pray something like this: Lord, I know I am human, and you are God. This situation is in the past. I claim victory over it and leave it all in your hands right now. I proclaim the power of the Holy Spirit over the situation right now. In Jesus's name, Amen!

- Verbally tell Satan to leave you alone. Get behind me, Satan; you have no control over my actions, thoughts, and behavior. God has forgiven this situation, and it is in the past. God is in control. I command you in the power of the Holy Spirit to leave!
- Praise God again and keep praising Him. He is giving you victory in this very moment through the power of the Holy Spirit.

One of my favorite sayings at church in Africa is, "Praise God, Praise God Again!" This phrase is often repeated throughout the service, especially in the beginning. I encourage you today to keep on praising God and rebuking Satan. Go to God's Word and read it. Read about people who God helped through difficult situations. Read the Psalms and begin to praise God in your heart for this victory. The point is to focus on God, not yourself or the past. I spent much time praying during my difficult times and dealing with forgiveness situations. I confessed to God that I am human and am struggling and that I need His help. Simply put, I am releasing the situation to God and depending on Him. And, as I do these things, I find myself being transformed by God.

Transformation by God

As I started doing things to help direct my mind back on God, not the problems or people stressing me out, He began to transform my life. The following is a graphic describing some things which helped me stay focused on God, not me. You see, as I prayed and started listening to God, I found there were things of God I needed to spend time doing. For example, Bible study. I started to spend time in God's Word, studying and learning, listening to the Bible on audio, and taking notes, and I even signed up for a free Old Testament class online. As I learned more about the Bible, I recognized how little I knew about God's Word. I would practice His presence in my life throughout the day. Focusing on these spiritual disciplines did wonders in my life! My thoughts became more focused on God. My actions improved. I did not spend time worrying or thinking of how someone had offended me. I started to think of ways to impact the world around me. I began to converse more with people in my surroundings. My relationships with others became more intimate than ever before. Everything changed when I started focusing on God and stayed focused on Him, not me. God truly transformed me spiritually, which also impacted me physically and mentally.

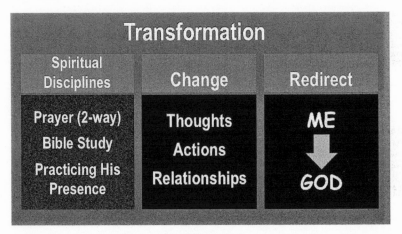

Transformation

Music has also been helpful to me and especially beneficial in directing my focus on God rather than myself. Since I grew up singing the old hymns, I find some worship songs or hymns online and play them. As I listen and sometimes sing along, this guides my attention and focus back to God, not me. I often discover peace, assurance, and rest in doing these things. As my heart becomes once again focused on God, how can I not praise Him? He helps me make daily decisions like this one to refocus on Him and not me. You have this too! God is waiting to hear from you. I know you will find peace as you depend on Jesus in these challenging situations. Take the chance and trust Him to help you find peace.

Summary

The sixth chapter delves into the topic of forgiving others. First, we talked about how to respond to unforgiving hearts. After this, we discussed being dependent on God for all our needs as we continue working toward forgiving others. The discussion included praising God and claiming victory over past relationship pains even when Satan directs our attention to these troubles. In this section, you were encouraged to present your needs to God and remain focused on Him, not yourself. We also discovered practical ways to help us redirect our attention to God.

Taking this step to forgive others is key to receiving forgiveness from God. Although it is not easy to get beyond our painful relationships and past injuries, we must be courageous. As we remember these new insights, let us stop and consider the following case study. After writing your response to the case study, move on to answer the questions. The questions are specifically designed to assist you in determining if you are ready to advance beyond your pain. I recommend you spend prayerful time considering each question, writing down your responses as you go.

Case Study Six

George has attended church for many years. Until recently, he was not serious about his relationship with God. But George has decided it is time to be serious about God. As George studied the Bible, he noticed scripture indicates that God can help him forgive others who have caused him mental anguish. George also knows that he has been distracted by things other than God. He wants to put all these things behind him today and stay focused on God. What advice will you offer George? How can God transform his life? What methods or things will help him stay focused on God, not other items? How will you help George understand God's forgiveness so that he can have peace with God, himself, and others?

My Response

Questions

1. Do I depend on God daily for His power in my life?

2. Do I trust Him with my problems and injured relationships?

3. Have I forgiven the people who injured me?

4. Have I chosen to put these pains behind me, or do they affect my life today?

5. Is my focus directed on myself or God?

6. How can I redirect my attention to God if it is on me?

7. Am I praising God and claiming victory over past injuries?

8. How is God transforming me today?

9. What can I do differently to allow Him to transform me more?

Notes

SEVEN

Moving On

being confident of this, that he who began a good work in you
will carry it on to completion until the day of Christ Jesus.
–Philippians 1:6

As you read this chapter, I hope you allow God to help you work
through past painful relationship injuries in your life. I also hope you are
feeling a bit of freedom from this experience. But now, how do you move
forward, consistently pursuing God and keeping the past remaining the
past? What happens when Satan reminds you of these experiences? How
will you respond? Chapter seven highlights several items that I hope are
helpful to you. First, we look at possible warning signs of unforgiveness.
Next, we look at biblical passages of encouragement. Following this
section, we dialogue about discovering ministry opportunities. First,
let us look at warning signs of unforgiveness.

Warning Signs of Unforgiveness

One way to identify whether you are moving beyond the painful
relationship injuries from the past is to assess your life for possible signs of
unforgiveness. Swartz classifies some unforgiveness indicators like "high

blood pressure, anxiety, depression…" and poor "immune response."[46] At first glance, these indicators appear to be physical symptoms, but they are closely intertwined with our mental and spiritual beings. For example, my blood pressure may be elevated (physical sign) when I am bitter toward someone (mental sign). And, if I refuse to release these pains to God, my spiritual journey is hindered (spiritual sign). If several symptoms are present, it could be an indication of unforgiveness. However, warning indicators may be occurring for reasons other than unforgiveness. Still, if signs are visible, it would be an excellent time to examine your life to determine whether unforgiveness exists in your heart. Once you identify if any unforgiveness exists, the next step is simple. Should you find unforgiveness in your heart, go back to the steps outlined in this book and repeat them.

Make a list of those you need to forgive. Then present these people to God. Ask God to help you release these pains to Him. Claim victory as you depend on God to advance beyond the pains. You may need to reconcile relationships. You may also need to forgive yourself. The goal is to get beyond this situation, where you release it all to God. As you receive God's forgiveness, offer forgiveness to others, and forgive yourself, you can expect to experience peace with God, yourself, and others. If you have forgiven all people, it is time to move on! I cannot imagine any better way to advance than to look at scriptures of encouragement as you claim victory and experience peace.

Biblical Encouragement

Scripture provides excellent nuggets of wisdom regarding handling conflict and forgiving others. In addition to the wisdom, the Bible offers examples of people whom God helped through difficult situations. I hope the following scripture verses bring encouragement and guidance to you concerning conflict and moving beyond your pain.

---

[46] Karen Swartz, "The Healing Power of Forgiveness," *Johns Hopkins' Health* no. 25 (Summer 2014): 8, accessed March 8, 2019, https://www.hopkinsmedicine. org/news/publications/johns_hopkins_health/files/sebindoc/u/z/F0CD31E9 34B955FC6F1E7D6135F98E73.pdf.

Old Testament Scriptures[47]

Starting a quarrel is like breaching a dam; so drop the matter before a dispute breaks out. – Proverbs 17:14

Do not be quickly provoked in your spirit, for anger resides in the lap of fools.
– Ecclesiastes 7:9

Do not seek revenge or bear a grudge against anyone among your people, but love your neighbor as yourself. I am the Lord.
–Leviticus 19:18

Pride goes before destruction, a haughty spirit before a fall.
–Proverbs 16:18

A gentle answer turns away wrath, but a harsh word stirs up anger.
–Proverbs 15:1

I, even I, am he who blots out your transgressions, for my own sake, and remembers your sins no more.
–Isaiah 43:25

The LORD will fight for you; you need only to be still.
–Exodus 14:14

Know therefore that the Lord your God is God; he is the faithful God, keeping his covenant of love to a thousand generations of those who love him and keep his commandments.
–Deuteronomy 7:9

---

[47] Taken from the *(NIV) Life Application Study Bible*.

New Testament Scriptures[48]

Everyone should be quick to listen, slow to speak and slow to become angry, because human anger does not produce the righteousness that God desires.
–James 1:19b–20

If it is possible, as far as it depends on you, live at peace with everyone.
–Romans 12:18

Make every effort to live in peace with everyone and to be holy; without holiness no one will see the Lord.
–Hebrews 12:14

Submit yourselves, then, to God. Resist the devil, and he will flee from you.
–James 4:7

Repent, then, and turn to God, so that your sins may be wiped out, that times of refreshing may come from the Lord,
–Acts 3:19

And when you stand praying, if you hold anything against anyone, forgive them, so that your Father in heaven may forgive you your sins.
–Mark 11:25

I can do all things through him who gives me strength.
–Philippians 4:13

Therefore, if anyone is in Christ, the new creation has come: The old has gone, the new is here!
–2 Corinthians 5:17

---

[48] Taken from the *(NIV) Life Application Study Bible.*

I trust these verses from the Bible provide some encouragement to you. As seen above and throughout scripture, God is faithful, but we must also do our part. As you grow in faith in Christ and continue moving beyond painful relationships, it is essential to discover opportunities to share God's love and this great news of forgiveness to others. Your testimony of how God is transforming your life and helping you get beyond the pain can benefit others. The following section in this chapter provides suggestions on impacting the world around you.

Seeking Opportunities

The following are a few ideas to seek opportunities to impact the world around you. Not all these suggestions will work in every community; however, it would not surprise me that you discover one or more work for you in your geographical area. I encourage you to select one or two and allow God to use your experiences to help others get beyond their pain too.

- Find a church that preaches the Bible and get involved.
- Find a group to connect with within your community.
- Seek opportunities to become friends with someone new.
- Visit a coffee shop and seek opportunities to make new acquaintances. Work on forming a new relationship.
- Call a friend or neighbor and share God's love with them.
- As you go shopping, find someone smiling, let them know their smile is contagious. Smile back!
- Go to a store and seek out someone needing help and help them.
- Write down your dreams and goals. Pursue at least one dream.
- Set new goals for reaching out to others. Set goals for two, five, eight, and ten years.
- Call your pastor/leader and notify them you are praying for them (and pray for them!).
- Find a place in your community where you can give back (homeless shelter, crisis center, local parks and recreation, food kitchen, foodbank).

- Make a list of positive things you see happening in your life.
- Spend a week volunteering at a Christian or other camp setting.
- Take a class and learn about a topic that would benefit your ministry or volunteer work.
- Donate food to a needy family.
- Volunteer to help clean up at your local restaurant.
- Volunteer at the local school or college.
- Spend a day praying and fasting for missionaries around the world.
- As you develop current relationships, share about the forgiveness you found in Christ and how He helped you get beyond past pains.
- Reach out to other people who are experiencing past pains. Point them to Christ, who can heal them and help them advance in their spiritual journey.

Numerous more opportunities could be available for you in your community to get involved. Pray about where God would like you to get involved, and then do it! Remember, seeking opportunities to do ministry sometimes means doing something uncomfortable or that seems unpleasant at the time. Smile as you follow through and see how God works in the lives around you! Read through the following case study and respond to the questions at the end. Make sure you record your response and be clear and specific in your answers.

Case Study Seven

Hannah realizes she is struggling in many ways. She has been having high blood pressure and is experiencing periodic depression. Recently Hannah has been getting sick, feeling tired, and often skips church. Her friends are starting to think there is something more serious going on with Hannah. She used to be more involved in church, go to the small group Bible study, and spend time with friends. Now, all Hannah can do is think about her situation, and she has no desire to be around other people. Who would have known that her own stepfather would rape and abuse her! Sometimes Hannah wonders if she will ever recover from these things in her life. Her mental anguish is immense, and she feels anger welling up inside herself. While she wants to be on good terms with God, herself, and others, finding her motivation for anything has been challenging. What is the root problem of Hannah's issues? What help will you provide her to aid her in getting on the right path and finding peace with God, herself, and others?

My Response

🎯 *Questions*

1. What are the warning signs of unforgiveness?

2. Do I identify any of these warning signs in my life currently?

3. Which Old Testament scripture is most helpful to me right now?

4. Which New Testament scripture is most helpful to me right now?

5. What opportunities do I see to minister in my community?

6. What is God asking me to do in my relationships, where I work and live?

Notes

EIGHT

Wrapping it Up

Finally, brothers and sisters, rejoice! Strive for full restoration,
encourage one another, be of one mind, live in peace.
And the God of love and peace will be with you.
−2 Corinthians 13:11

We have covered much information in the above chapters about ways to seek forgiveness and find peace with God, yourself, and others. We have offered hope and methods to get beyond the mental anguish caused by relationship injuries. Still, only you can decide whether to apply the principles to your life. So, what is God asking of you? How can you seek to help others experiencing similar damaged relationship pains? Chapter two uncovered the biblical understanding of forgiveness, which indicates releasing, letting things go, and freeing. We learned lessons from the Israelites, such as:

- God has great compassion, love, grace, mercy, and patience for His people.
- Efforts were essential by the Israelites to restore their relationship with God. They were expected to act in response to God's call.
- God's acts of forgiveness follow their choice to seek Him. As the Israelites seek God and repent, He demonstrates forgiveness.

- God's ability to restore brokenness when people seek Him. God is ready and able to restore broken relationships between Him and His children.
- God's power is available daily as people trust and depend on Him. He is ready to use His power as we trust in Him.
- God's constant pursuit of His people and triumph over sin. He never gives up on us. He continues to pursue us even when we are distant from Him.

We also learned lessons from Jesus concerning forgiveness. We saw Him offering forgiveness even as He was dying painfully on the cross. His storytelling exhibited the value of forgiving others and the effect of an unforgiving person. Although there are many lessons to learn from Jesus on forgiveness, here are some notable items we discussed:

- Christ illustrates His immense love for humanity, even while enduring great pain.
- Humility before God and showing remorse for sins are relevant to salvation.
- Jesus displayed and valued love, peace, forgiveness, and reconciliation.
- Forgiveness of others must be genuine and from the heart.
- We must forgive as many times as necessary.
- We should stop living carelessly on our own resources and seek God for forgiveness.
- Jesus Christ is ready and waiting with open arms for us to return to Him.
- We should rejoice with those who return to Christ.
- Jealousy and pride are obstacles to humility and obstruct forgiveness.
- God knows our hearts and behaviors; we cannot trick Him.
- God expects behavioral change following forgiveness.

The second chapter wraps up with a discussion on worldviews and perspectives. We talked about how our view of God influences how we perceive He interacts with us.

In the third chapter, we made a list of potential people needing forgiveness from us. We identified these people determining which ones might be creating painful emotions or memories. Then we removed people from the list who did not create painful emotions. Following this, we identified specific incidents/issues of those remaining on the list. After we completed our list, we acknowledged limitations that are out of our control, such as:

- **Physical Limitations**. Due to geographical distance, death, or other reasons, I cannot connect to some people causing me pain. I must accept this as a limitation.
- **Mental Limitations**. I cannot truly grasp how people think or why they think the way they do. I cannot change this. I cannot read minds or entirely understand their worldview as I did not live their lives. I must accept this as a limitation.
- **Spiritual Limitations.** People are at different spiritual levels. Some are Christians; others proclaim Christianity while not behaving in what we perceive as appropriate Christian behavior. I must accept and recognize that I do not know the spiritual maturity level of others, and I cannot change this. I am limited to such knowledge.
- **I may not be right**. For some people, this is tough to accept. You and I have met people who are always right about things. Are you a person who perceives you are always right? Think again; you are not always right about everything since you are human. Everyone makes mistakes; get over it, move on. We learn from our mistakes. This limitation exists because of our humanity.

We also identified expectations by using the following methods of inquiry:

- **Physical Expectations.** Ask yourself, how do I expect people to respond to me? Do I anticipate them responding by punching me in the face or stomping their feet? Do I believe they will stay quiet and not say anything? Do I expect them to withdraw physically? Do I anticipate crying or harsh words? What about nonverbal reactions? What looks will I receive from them? What physical (verbal and nonverbal) expectations do I have of people?

- **Mental Expectations.** Do I anticipate others will hold a grudge against me? Should I expect them to be distant or distracted mentally when we talk again? What about trust? Do I expect them to trust me? How can I anticipate them responding the next time mentally compared to our previous encounters?

- **Spiritual Expectations.** It may be the most challenging for Christians to accept. We have specific ways we believe others should behave as Christians. We expect all believers to be on the same level that we perceive them to be. Sometimes we think church, organizations, or group leaders should have a deeper spiritual maturity level than others. It may be accurate for some, but certainly not for all. These are our spiritual expectations of others.

In the fourth chapter, we focused on recognizing and experiencing God's power. We examined how our perspective of God influences our perception of Him working in our lives. We considered experiencing His transforming power by praising, reading, and studying scripture, praying, practicing God's presence, and seeking personal forgiveness from Him. We asked these questions to aid us in discovering how we perceive God and experience His power:

1. What is my perspective of God?
2. How involved do I expect Him to be in my life?
3. In what ways am I experiencing God's power?
4. Am I experiencing His power daily?
5. Do I truly recognize the power of God?
6. Do I know and accept in my heart that God is more powerful than problems of the past?
7. Am I willing to release them into His power?
8. Am I pursuing God with all I have?
9. What ways help me to connect to God and praise Him?

In the fifth chapter, we examined how to experience personal forgiveness. We talked about how Christ's death and resurrection provide all we need to overcome the past pains. We also presented the following guidelines in helping us reach out to Jesus for forgiveness:

- **Praise Him:** Because He is God and deserves praises. You might say something like this: Hey God, you are marvelous and deserve praises. I praise you just because of who you are. I acknowledge you are powerful and able to forgive.
- **Thank Him in Advance for Answering Prayer:** God, I know you hear and answer my prayers today. Thank you for this right now.
- **Acknowledge Your Limitations/Expectations:** Lord Jesus, I know that I have physical, mental, and spiritual limitations. I realize my expectations are not always correct. I was born with sin, and because I am human, I make mistakes. But I have faith in you. Hear my cry today.
- **Ask God to Forgive Any Sins:** God, I realize you offer me forgiveness. You have paid the ultimate price on the cross, and I accept this gift of love from you, which covers my sin. I have sinned; please forgive me.
- **Accept His forgiveness:** Lord, even though I cannot completely understand your grace and all the love you have for me through your death on the cross, I know you have given me grace today. I accept your gift of forgiveness and claim it right now. I know you will guide me in the coming days.
- **Praise God for His Grace and Forgiveness to You:** Father, I praise you because you have forgiven me of my sins right now and given me grace. Lord, I praise you because I know you are in control of my life. I praise you, God because I know you will help me grow deeper in you. I praise you, God, that I will sleep well tonight knowing you are in control of everything. Amen!

The final section in the fifth chapter provided a bit of information on how we need to forgive ourselves for the past pains and hurts, whether we caused them or someone else caused them to occur.

In the sixth chapter, our topic was forgiveness of others. We conversed about how a Christian should respond to unforgiving hearts. After this, we discussed being dependent on God for all our needs to forgive others. The dialogue included praising God and claiming victory over past relationship pains even when Satan directs our attention to these troubles. We also talked about the following steps to help you focus on God and not on the past.

- Praise God for who He is.
- Praise God for helping you overcome past injuries.
- Claim victory over this situation in Christ. You might wish to pray something like this: Lord, I know I am human, and you are God. This situation is in the past. I claim victory over it and leave it all in your hands right now. I proclaim the power of the Holy Spirit over the situation right now. In Jesus's name, Amen!
- Verbally tell Satan to leave you alone. Get behind me, Satan; you have no control over my actions, thoughts, and behavior. God has forgiven this situation, and it is in the past. God is in control. I command you in the power of the Holy Spirit to leave!
- Praise God again and keep praising God. He is giving you victory in this very moment through the power of the Holy Spirit.

The last section of this chapter featured my encounter with God in Africa. I conveyed experiences of how I became dependent on God for all my needs while there. The encounter with Him revolutionized and changed my thoughts, actions, and relationships. The chapter concluded with an emphasis on directing and keeping our focus on God, not ourselves, to overcome painful memories and past experiences.

In the seventh chapter, we examined some methods of moving on beyond the past and painful relationship experiences. We looked for physical, mental, and spiritual warning signs that unforgiveness might be present in our lives. We focused on encouragement through both Old and New Testaments scriptures. Finally, we talked about seeking ministry opportunities to share with others and help them get beyond their pains. The following are some ideas we discussed:

- Seek opportunities to become friends with someone new.
- Visit a coffee shop and seek opportunities to make new acquaintances. Work on forming a new relationship.
- Go to a store and seek out someone needing help and help them.
- Set new goals for reaching out to others. Set goals for two, five, eight, and ten years.
- Make a list of positive things you see happening in your life.
- Take a class and learn about a topic that would benefit your ministry or volunteer work.
- As you develop current relationships, share about the forgiveness you found in Christ and how He helped you get beyond past pains.

I encourage you to seek God daily; He will meet you where you are. He is faithful, but you must do your part too. Choose to move forward in your relationship with God and others. We are reminded in 1 Peter 5:7 to "Cast all your anxiety on him because he cares for you." You can get beyond the pains of the past as you embark on this exciting new journey with God. I pray you will find peace with God, yourself, and others as He transforms your life into something new each day.

Notes

BIBLIOGRAPHY

Berthoud, Pierre. "The Reconciliation of Joseph With His Brothers Sin, Forgiveness And Providence, Genesis 45:1–11 (42:1–45:11) and 50:15–21," *European Journal of Theology* 17, no. 1 (2008): 8, accessed March 30, 2019. http://web.a.ebscohost.com/ehost/pdfviewer/pdfviewer?vid=4&sid=d22f8362-436c-4fb4-9c5f-c81a4eda769d%40sessionmgr4006.

Calhoun, Adele Ahlberg. *Spiritual Disciplines Handbook: Practices That Transform Us,* (InterVarsity Press, 2005), Kindle.

Domeris, William R. "Biblical Perspectives on Forgiveness," Journal *of Theology for Southern Africa* 54 (March 1986): 48–50. Accessed January 8, 2019. http://web.b.ebscohost.com/ehost/pdfviewer/pdfviewer?vid=4&sid=8694c753-4baf-4760-a05b-5e601d0f109d%40pdc-v-sessmgr03.

Haimovitz, Kyla and Carol S. Dweck. "The Origins of Children's Growth and Fixed Mindsets: New Research and a New Proposal," *Child Development* 88 no. 6 (2017): 1849. https://doi.org/10.1111/cdev.12955

Logos Bible Software, *Bible Word Study Guide,* (s.v. "forgive," "forgiveness," "reconcile," "reconciliation," "repent," "repentance"). V. 9.5 SR-19.5.0.0019. Faithlife. PC. 2021.

Mininger, Marcus A. "A God-Centered Ministry and Responses to Conflict Between Peers: Perspectives From the Apostle

Paul," *Mid-America Journal of Theology* 27 (2016): 125–130, accessed November 18, 2019. http://web.a.ebscohost.com/ehost/pdfviewer/pdfviewer?vid=11&sid=c3f259f9-0982-493b-9bfb-a16f97775659%40sessionmgr4008.

Rockwell, Stephen. "Faith, Hope and Love in the Colossian Epistle," *The Reformed Theological Review* 72, no. 1 (April 2013): 44, accessed February 20, 2019, http://web.b.ebscohost.com/ehost/pdfviewer/pdfviewer?vid=4&sid=08a6810e-64d2-4cac-adbb-e25cce18c293%40pdc-v-sessmgr01.

Swartz, Karen. "The Healing Power of Forgiveness," *Johns Hopkins' Health* no. 25 (Summer 2014): 8, accessed March 8, 2019. https://www.hopkinsmedicine.org/news/publications/johns_hopkins_health/files/sebindoc/u/z/F0CD31E934B955FC6F1E7D6135F98E73.pdf.

"The Colossian Heresy," *(NIV) Life Application Study Bible*, (following Col. 1:14).

Tran, John C. W. *Authentic Forgiveness* (Global Perspectives Series), (Langham Creative Projects, Canada: Langham Publishing, 2020), Kindle.

RESOURCES FOR FURTHER
EXPLORATION AND HELP

Getting to Know God
https://peacewithgod.net/?dr=peacewithgod.org
https://www.cru.org/us/en/how-to-know-god/would-you-like-to-know-god-personally/faqs/resources-for-the-spiritually-curious.html

Forgiveness
https://www.evworthington-forgiveness.com/
https://www.psychologytoday.com/us/basics/forgiveness

Spiritual Disciplines
https://www.contemplativeoutreach.org/centering-prayer-method/
https://www.pdfdrive.com/spiritual-disciplines-handbook-practices-that-transform-us-e195129642.html

Peace and Relationships
https://rw360values.org/
https://www.amazon.com/Peacemaker-Biblical-Resolving-Personal-Conflict/dp/0801064856